What About Me?

By Dr. R. Alan Seamons

What About Me?

Virtue Based Training and the SamiTales Program

This book of instruction is to accompany the training of the *8 Virtues* in the *SamiTales Series*. It establishes a common set of terms and objectives for assisting individuals in the quest to live a virtuous life and attain personal peace. It is an abridged version of the *Child of Virtue Manual* and a companion to the teacher training workbook *It's All Up to Me* and the *Child of Virtue Student Handbook*.

© 2011 Ray Alan Seamons

All rights reserved. No part of this book may be reproduced in any form or by any means without permission in writing from the publisher, **SamiTales**.

ISBN   978-1-936799-54-1

Contents

Introduction 1
    Example 1
    Teaching and Learning.. 4
Chapter 1 *What's in it for me?* 7
    Success... 9
Chapter 2 *Why children?* 18
    Example 20
    Teaching and Learning.. 21
    Safety and Security 22
Chapter 3 *Why is it so difficult?* 24
    Survival.. 25
    Society 27
    Ego 28
    Competition 29
Chapter 4 *What is virtuous living?* 33
    Fundamental Construct... 36
Chapter 5 *How does it work?* 41
    Hierarchical Structure 42
    Interconnection 42
    Cyclical Nature 47
    Target Audience 49
    Academic Presentation 50
Chapter 6 *What is the CORE Virtue?* 53
    HUMILITY.. 54

Chapter 7 *What are the FOUNDATIONAL Virtues?* 59
    COURAGE 60
    CLEANLINESS 64
    OBEDIENCE 68
    INDUSTRY   Foundational Virtue 72

Chapter 8 *What are the POWER Virtues?* 77
    INTEGRITY 78
    WISDOM 82

Chapter 9 *What is the SUSTAINING Virtue?* 87
    GRATITUDE 88

Chapter 10 *What is the GOAL?* 93
    Peace Must Be Our Purpose! 94
    Personal Peace 95
    Peace Progression 97

Chapter 11 *What is the program?* 102
    The Evolution of SamiTales 102
    SamiTales Program of 8 Virtues Training 104
    Child of Virtue 106

Chapter 12 *What can I do?* 108
    Children: A DECLARATION of Rights 111
    MOMs: A DECLARATION to the World 112
    MOMMIES ARE FOREVER 112

References 115

FOREWORD

The author of this work openly acknowledges and offers grateful thanks to all those involved in the "great conversation" that has occurred over the course of time. Specifically, love, gratitude, and respect is given to my dear wife, Karen, without whom these thoughts would have never materialized.

In the process of sharing insights, one must ask, are there truly any original thoughts or ideas? Are words merely personalized adaptations of previously conceived insights? The thoughts assembled in this work are a compilation of years of education and training, reading and reflection with a variety of educators, collaborators and scholars, mixed with the wisdom of ordinary, seemingly common individuals. This work is a byproduct of those who came before and is presented by way of suggestion for personal evaluation. It is intended to increase personal awareness through self reflection and honesty. The greatest challenge in organizing it has been the personal confrontation with who I am against the new standard. Continuous self improvement leading to personal peace is the ultimate goal

Introduction

**Knowing others is intelligence;
Knowing yourself is true wisdom.
Mastering others is strength,
Mastering yourself is true power.**

From Tao Te Ching by Laozi (6th Century BC)

- Why are the lusts of greed and excesses of gluttony ruling our lives?
- Why is peace so elusive, but wrath and war appealing?
- Where is our future?
- How will we change the tide of current events?
- Where do I begin?

Awakening

As a father of a large family, and having been engaged in youth training and development all of my life, I have always been sensitive to the challenges of childhood. Initially isolated in my typical middle income American world, it wasn't until I became involved with the national organization called *Big Brothers of America* that I began to challenge my age old perspective and inherent bias of the educated white male. One of my children-at-risk with *Big Brothers* was Alex. He was the second oldest of eight children, each of whom had a different father. Alex's older brother used drugs and sold them in order to afford his habit. His employment history was spotty, and to survive he engaged in petty theft and the subsequent sale of the stolen items. This brother was a very nice, personable kid who unfortunately got caught up in a system that was unable to meet his needs. The whole family, less the older brother, lived in a two-bedroom apartment where survival was the first order of business.

My objective as a *Big Brother* to Alex was to ensure that he was drug free through to his 16th birthday while he finished his success-based probation-enforced recovery training. Alex was sexually active and had used drugs since age 12. He had sold and used every drug on the streets but was fortunate enough to enjoy cheap marijuana the most; this helped him avoid the devastating cycle of hard drugs. To survive in this most difficult social environment, Alex was a member of a gang. In his short life he had already witnessed two shootings.

During our first meeting, Alex introduced me to eight distinct gangs that roamed the neighborhood where he lived. As it turned out, the gang was, in reality, his family. You join a gang, I learned, for safety, security, and social connection. His biological family was important, but it was his gang family that was vital. Alex loved and admired his older brother, and this connection created his most difficult challenge as it was his desire to be just like him. My job was to broaden his perspective so as to avoid the rut that had been forged through the example of this older brother. Fortunately, Alex was bright and wanted to improve his future. He was an excellent student, which he attributed to being high on marijuana during most class periods. It is important to place this experience into perspective. We are not talking about inner-city New York, Harlem, Watts, or even East LA. This was in a relatively small, extremely conservative, family orientated, mid-western American city. In a discussion of national gang problems and the evils of the inner-city life, this would definitely not be in the top-10 list of children-at-risk locations.

Gratefully I report that my simple involvement with Alex had some positive impact. He successfully completed his recovery training, he remained drug-free, and he advanced to high school. Alex is the exception, not the norm. I provided a trusted adult reference for Alex to bounce off thoughts and decisions. It wasn't formal accountability, but at least it provided some emotional responsibility for his impulses and choices. He gained understanding and respect for my value system regardless of whether he incorporated these values or not.

This whole experience rocked my simple world. I began to realize that for much of my life I had lived in a protected capsule, and my idealistic thoughts and opinions were distorted accordingly. My view was through rose-colored glasses. Following this experience I began to run other scenarios. What of the true inner-city gangland children-at-risk? Where do they turn for counsel and advice? More importantly, what is the source of their value training? Where do their core virtues come from?

Time has passed since this experience, but similar concerns continue to surface with the only variation being that of the population being considered. America has a mere 74 million children and 70% of them live with two parents. Of those not living with two parents, 26% live with one parent. Of the remaining 4%, half live with a grandparent and the rest are street children. Europe and Asia have similar numbers with similar demographics. But, what of the nearly 200 million children in China or the 150 million in India? Or how about the kids in the former Soviet Republic or South America? Even more concerning are the war-ravaged countries of Africa and the Middle East. What values are being taught formally or otherwise to the children in the developing countries of the world? These populations make the challenges of the inner-city kids look simple by comparison. As I contemplate the needs of so many at-risk children, I am completely overwhelmed and consumed by the urgency and magnitude of this condition.

There is hope, however, because somewhere in the process of helping one at-risk child, my life changed forever. Gone are my preoccupations with petty personal problems and concerns. Gone are my whiny days and the anxiety I feel over family inconveniences. Gone is my toleration for excess, indulgence, and entitlement. Quieted now, I sit feeling frustrated, sad, overwhelmed, and neutralized. Why, in this time of global prosperity and abundance enabled by ever-changing technology, are the lusts of greed and the excesses of gluttony ruling our lives? Why is peace so elusive but wrath and war so appealing? Where is our future? How will we change the tide of current events? It was a quote by Mother Teresa that got me focused again: "If you can't feed a hundred people, then feed just one." Where do I begin? Who do I assist? What is to be done? Who will choose to become engaged? The only person that I have power over is me, and so I will begin with personal self-control. Once I become master of myself I will be in a position to assist others.

As I continue to wrestle with my thoughts and feelings regarding at-risk children, I have utilized my education, experience, and insights in an effort to identify the critical factors at play in the possible solution to this situation. Greater than meeting the physical needs of food and shelter, my focus begins with the underlying motivators of human behavior. In frustration I wonder, why can't we all just get along? Are we genetically prone to animosity and aggression? Is it awareness that is needed? Would a common perspective and shared understanding lead to increased tolerance and compassion? Such questions led me to identify virtues that I feel are time proven and universal, and that seem to be elusive in our current society, but which may possibly curb the negative influences surrounding us. I have considered the current vehicles of education and communication available to disseminate such pearls of wisdom to others. These thoughts led to the phrase, **"Child of Virtue, Peace is My Purpose."** This axiom surfaced with forceful impact because such an individual can influence not only his/her personal existence, but also that of all people encountered in the journey of life.

Engagement

As a child of the universe, I seek for harmony within myself and within the world around me. As I come to know myself and control myself, I naturally develop the desire to acquire virtues that ultimately lead to personal harmony and peace. This peace removes all tethers that bind me, allowing for ultimate freedom and continued growth and improvement. As a Child of Virtue, peace is my purpose regardless of age, gender, nationality, race, or any other brand that seeks to label and define my existence. Peace in action is standing up to fear.

**A life of peace, purity, and refinement leads to
a calm and untroubled old age.**
Cicero (106 BC – 43 BC)

The intent of this endeavor is to provide a solid foundation from which to instruct the "virtues of the ages" to the children of the world with an end objective of personal peace leading to greater global contentment. The 8 Virtues include: Humility, Courage, Cleanliness, Obedience, Industry, Integrity, Wisdom, and Gratitude. Peace becomes the crowning achievement of virtuous living.

The suggestions for self help contained in the following pages are for all of us. The greatest challenge in writing them down was in the personal confrontation with my own inadequacies. Personal refinement is painful for we become both the sculptor as well as the clay. Please recognize that I am not preaching here, but learning as I seek to apply these virtues into my own life.

This handbook is designed to be practical and useful.

- *Chapter 1 is an unassuming assessment of the power of delayed gratification, which is the key to success. Included is a discussion on obedience and integrity. The lack of cognitive dissonance is the key to peace of mind, and peace of mind leads to peace on earth.*
- *Chapter 2 validates the importance of children in changing the world. The emerging needs of the children of the Millennial Generation begin with virtue training.*
- *Chapter 3 discusses opposition, ego mastery, humility and pride. Delayed gratification leads to success, but mastery of thoughts leads to peace.*
- *Chapter 4 addresses the components of a virtuous life, the importance of personal continuous improvement, and the concepts of personal authenticity/integrity. It is here that the 8 Virtues are acknowledged in a formal manner.*
- *Chapter 5 talks about the 8 Virtues and the importance of their interrelationship. The characteristics that set this pro-*

- *gram apart from other similar courses are presented.*
- *Chapters 6 through 9 present the 8 Virtues in detail.*
- *Chapter 10 defines peace as the reward of virtuous living, and establishes this as a universal goal.*
- *Chapter 11 presents the history of the SamiTales Program, its Mission, and Vision.*
- *Chapter 12 is a call to action.*

**If you can't feed a hundred people, then feed just one....
We shall never know all the good
that a simple smile can do.**
Mother Teresa (1910-1997)

Chapter 1

What's in it for me?

The highest purpose of intellectual cultivation is to give a man a perfect knowledge and mastery of his own inner self; to render our consciousness its own light and its own mirror.
Frederich Leopold von Hardenberg (1772-1801)

- *Success and peace are two objectives in life; both require delayed gratification.*
- *Honesty is a continuum of obedience to integrity.*
- *While peace of mind is success, success does not guarantee peace of mind.*
- *Peace is the absence of cognitive dissonance. It is a state of mind based upon honesty and integrity in all aspects of life.*
- *Personal peace is a progression of continuous improvement.*

Caught up in this very long thought, I have arrived at the following conclusion. For most people, there are two objectives in life: one is the attainment of success, and the other is peace of mind.

The age old process of success involves the steps of commitment, planning, obedience, and hard work. Although these names may change by culture or era, the sentiment remains the same. Success is personally defined and may or may not be for the betterment of anyone other than the individual. Regardless of the motivation, success is based upon delayed gratification. Success is driven from and leads to pride: pride in accomplishments, pride in attainments, and pride in achievements. The greatest obstacle to success is fear of failure.

While peace of mind is a form of success, success does not necessarily equate to peace of mind. It appears to me that honesty is the deciding factor. The most basic form of honesty is that of blind obedience. At this level, we obey to avoid punishment, or to receive benefits. This basic level of honesty is required to succeed. At a higher level is integrity, or honesty with self. Consistency between word and action is a start to personal integrity, but it goes even deeper to include consistency between action and thought. Weak men obey out of fear, but honest men obey out of honor and respect. The quest for peace begins here.

The skills of success, once mastered, become the building blocks of this higher order. The mind of the truly honest man is free from the discomfort of holding conflicting ideas, allowing for greater wisdom. It seems that as behavior and intent align, wisdom is naturally generated. As with any muscle, the more it is stretched and fatigued, the stronger is grows. Building personal integrity is the same; it isn't attained overnight. It isn't something that is achieved without setback. It isn't like a math test where the answers, although challenging, can be aced. It is a grand mission for life and any degree of achievement is a huge step towards serenity. A natural byproduct of true integrity and mature thinking is gratitude. A mind free from the conflict of opposing thoughts and associated guilt is a healthy mind open to prudent thought. Astute thought naturally leads to feelings of gratitude for those who have assisted in the climb. Even grander than gratitude for success is a sense of appreciation for all experiences, even the challenging and the sad. Gratitude grows from humility, and humility cultivates gratitude.

It takes humility to foster integrity. Humility is a candid assessment of personal strengths and weaknesses. Humility manages pride, and facilitates the quest for integrity. Unmanaged pride and vanity feed on success and, left unregulated, can become overbearing, dominating, and cruel. This quest for peace of mind confronts all of us at some point in the sojourn of life. Some event, either external or internal, awakens us to desire peace. Once humbled, we may choose to bind our ego and police our pride from then on. How much better off we all would be if we learned to control our pride as it is young and growing instead of when it is fully mature and dominating. How much happier we all would be if we avoided the pitfalls of unguarded pride in our climb to success. How much more valuable would we all would be to those who surround us if we had established as our goal in the beginning, "success with peace of mind."

Success

How do I become successful? In short, success is based on delayed gratification: postponing the desires and pleasures of the moment for a greater tomorrow. The four skills for success are: commit, plan, obey, and work. These directly correspond to the virtues of: courage, cleanliness, obedience, and industry.

SUCCESS PROCESS

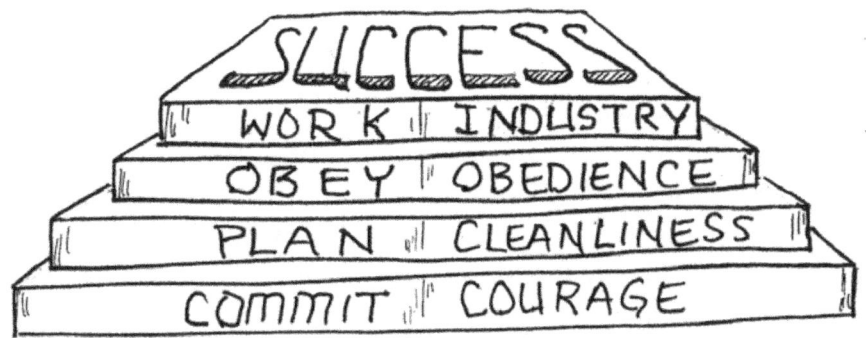

Commit/Courage

Success starts with personal commitment. It takes courage and patience to commit to delay the impulses of the moment. It takes courage to envision a life beyond the current existence. It takes courage to order the events necessary to achieve this desired life. It takes courage to comply to the requirements of an ordered plan. It takes courage and patience to put in the sustained effort necessary to achieve the skills, knowledge, and discipline needed. As mentioned before, delayed gratification is fundamental to the success process. It takes courage in the heat of the moment to delay this gratification of the moment. Courage is the predetermined commitment to resist distractive, destructive, and unhealthy impulses and situations. We need courage to plan, courage to improve, and courage to stand. Courageous people can still be filled with fear. Courage, therefore, is not the lack of fear, but the ability to master fear.

Plan/Cleanliness

The first step in planning for success is recognizing that there is a grander future beyond the current path, and that although desired, it will not be achieved without effort. It must be understood that this grander future can only be achieved through conscious exertion and work. The process is then identified and a plan developed that estimates the cost and sacrifices required. Once this big picture is in place, it must be resolved to not deviate. Setbacks come, but the big picture must be retained. Envision yourself as if you have already attained the goal. Picture yourself enjoying the rewards of our hard work. Internalize it, burn it into your subconscious for when the impulses hit and the desire to take the easy road surfaces, we will need the courage to recall why we are holding strong, why we are resisting.

Cleanliness is order in our environment, order in our society, and order in our thinking. Order maximizes thought, growth, and improvement. Life is not a random occurrence, and taking charge of it requires planning and order. Chaos is the end result of allowing circumstances to rule. A clean well fed body living in a sanitary environment creates the ideal place to expand thoughts and increase abilities.

Obey/Obedience

Obedience is the resolve to obey and to follow a pre-determined plan regulated either by yourself or by society. Obedience is the requirement to receive the protection of justice within society. If the safety, security, and advantages of a collective group are desired, then adhering to those same rules is required. Deviation from the predetermined societal plan leads to anarchy and disorder. Each desired attainment, such as degrees, honors and certificates, comes with it requirements that demand compliance. We may get away with disobedience once in a while, but ultimately accountability will be required.

Work/Industry

Without hard work against a predetermined plan, we will have gained nothing. All the planning in the world is pointless without work. Struggle is the source of genius. Nothing of value comes easy. It is in the trenches that additional insights are gained and increased courage attained to provide the energy and fortitude to achieve goals. In this process of taking charge of life, unimagined opportunities will present themselves as character is built. As with any skill, time and practice results in personal improvement. Cycling through this improvement process refines our very being. This is called continuous improvement. Once mastered, the on-going improvement process can and will be utilized on anything and everything engaged in. Success can be ours in anything we desire if we have the patience to delay the gratification of the moment.

Peace

These four skills will lead to success, but success alone does not automatically result in peace. Peace is a state of mind based upon honesty and integrity in all aspects of life. It is more than obedience to avoid punishment and promote justice. Integrity is delaying the gratification of the moment for a greater tomorrow. It is doing the right thing for the right reason. Peace emerges with this higher level of thought. Integrity eliminates mental conflicts allowing for greater wisdom. Wisdom, in turn, leads to feelings of gratitude for all things.

We each desire success. As a culture, people, and world, the drive for advancement is inborn. Once successful, there is yet another choice to be made, either consciously or unconsciously. Success, left unchecked, leads to greed, wrath, and envy, all of which are outgrowths of vanity. The fear of losing what we have achieved and attained, grown in the spirit of scarcity, drives us all to naturally hold on to things. Fear breeds fear. The oldest and strongest emotion of mankind is fear. It is a distressing emotion initiated by a perceived threat. Fear triggers the "fight or flight" response. Fear is, in reality, False Evidence Appearing Real.

PEACE PROCESS

We vainly compare, we greedily take, we gluttonously collect, we enviously achieve, and we wrathfully control, all in pursuit of security and satisfaction. To lust for more is seen as being better. In this paradigm, taking is immediate and satisfying, while giving is absurd. The tools of success are confronted with the challenge of integrity and honesty. Success develops pride, but vanity-driven pride blocks humility. Wisdom is only attained through the gateway of integrity. Gratitude is a by-product of wisdom. We can practice integrity, wisdom, gratitude and even peace, but until true integrity is mastered, wisdom and gratitude will not flow naturally. It is then, and only then, that true peace, peace with self, is achieved.

As a society we have been deceived. Playing upon our vanities, the marketing folks have convinced us all that bigger, newer, faster, and safer is always better. They have successfully sold us, amid our ever growing egos, on the belief that satisfaction and contentment are directly tied to acquisition, impact, achievement, and control. This just isn't true. History shows that it never has been true and the current world condition indicates that it won't be true in the future either. Discontent is the byproduct of this type of reasoning. This scarcity mentality ensures that we never feel that we have enough: enough money, enough toys, enough possessions, enough security, enough attention, and enough significance. As such, we all compete for limited resources in an attempt to feel safe and appreciated. The reality is that there is sufficient for all. The reality is that contentment and satisfaction are not found in things. The reality is that contentment is a state of mind attained only though success and peace. Happiness is not secured through ease, but through self-mastery. Peace is the reward of virtuous living.

Honesty is not a stagnant point of arrival. It is a gradual scale from simple to sophisticated, from social to personal. On this honesty continuum of obedience to integrity, obedience is the lowest level. We obey for the reward of group protection, or to avoid punishment. At best, this stage of social honesty is at a compliance level only. Often it's just about not getting caught. For example, acts of deception, manipulation, hypocrisy, and intentional distortion can function quite well alongside a standard of mere social compliance. However, performing at this base level while simultaneously holding the loftier aspirations of integrity will result in mental discomfort. Cognitive dissonance is the psychological term used to describe this condition. Integrity is more than honesty. Integrity is the elimination of the cognitive dissonance that is associated with manipulation, deceit, and justification. True personal honesty or integrity lies within the center of our soul. Integrity is being honest when others do not see. This includes honesty with others but, more importantly, it is honesty with self. Integrity is consistency between word and deed, between thought and action, and between intent and behavior.

Wisdom is clear, mature reasoning. This kind of thinking is only available to the mind that is unencumbered with deceit, and is void of cognitive dissonance. Wise people are in a position to balance pride and humility, and this allows for sufficient confidence to excel, as well as to forgive and serve others. Wise people know that they are only successful because of the gifts and sacrifices of many others, past and present.

We must be careful not to confuse wisdom with the academic acquisition of knowledge. Education and learning are worthy endeavors, but when mastery is taken to the extreme it generally results in power and control over people and the elements, but rarely over self. Wisdom dictates that the end result of personal development should be submission, but this is rejected by the vast majority because it directly opposes success and control. The wise individual learns the power of self control and this is where peace begins.

Peace lives in the house of wisdom, and wisdom is unattainable without integrity through the minimization and elimination of cognitive dissonance. The skills of courage, obedience, and industry do not, in and of themselves, lead to peace, wisdom, or integrity. It is true that wisdom, integrity, and peace are all based upon courage, obedience, and industry, but possessing these traits does not ensure wisdom. Wisdom grows in direct proportion to the absence of cognitive dissonance. Gratitude is the awareness and acknowledgement that no one is self-made, that everyone has a mentor, and that even the hardships encountered have been positive in personal development because they have forged us into who we are. Gratitude for all circumstances is the sign of a mature person. All things endured with the right perspective can be beneficial. Gratitude is the sustaining component of the entire process leading to peace. Such gratitude includes thanksgiving for all circumstances and conditions of life, not just the positive. Such gratitude is openly and abundantly dispersed. Such gratitude fosters humility. It is recognition to everyone for everything.

Freed from the mental suffering of cognitive dissonance thoughts of wisdom and gratitude are strengthened. The mind is freed to discover peace. Not like the lighting of a dark room with a flip of the switch, peace comes slowly and concisely one step at a time. Like the majesty of the sun rising slowly but steadily over the hills and plains, the personal peace progress is gradual and consistent. It is a cyclical process of continuous improvement, each turn of the wheel resulting in greater personal refinement expanding contentment and increased serenity. This is the ultimate goal: peace with self, peace with surroundings, peace with others!

When something is authentic it is considered genuine and timeless. A replica is never as valuable as the "real thing." As people we tend to develop two identities: the public image and the private one. Likewise, we see ourselves differently than others see us. Authenticity is the degree of reality between these two perspectives. Personal perspectives are developed over time based upon observable attitudes and behaviors.

Discovering and accepting where we are is more important than where we actually are. We must begin here, in the present. This isn't competition and it's not a race; it is a totally one-on-one assessment. The suggestions for self help contained in the following pages are for all of us. The greatest challenge for me when creating this assessment was in the actual confrontation with myself. Personal refinement is painful for we become both the sculptor as well as the clay. Please recognize that I am not preaching here, but learning as I grow.

By design, as we progress further, we are placing ourselves in an uncomfortable situation. We will have to reassess where we fit with this new perspective. It becomes a personal challenge begging for maturity.

The mature person will persevere because they will see how the growth will transpire through challenging, long-held paradigms. In discussing some of these simple connections I feel challenged, overwhelmed, and embarrassed. As Carl Rogers stated, "The curious paradox is that when I accept myself just as I am, then I can change."

There are visible behavioral attributes associated with each of the virtues described. The 8 Virtue Attributes Assessment on the following page is a simple method of "checking your oil" regarding personal attributes that are associated with the given virtues. It is to be used often to measure your progress.

What's in it for me?
Peace is the reward of virtuous living.
Peace is a clear conscience.
Peace is tolerance and order.
Peace is unconditional acceptance.
Peace is compassion.
Peace is the absence of fear.
Peace is worth the effort.

ATTRIBUTE ASSESSMENT

Mark each statement as it applies to you: 1 never   2 occassionally   3 often   4 frequently   5 always

Humility
___ 1. I am meek and forgiving.
___ 2. I accept constructive feedback from others.
___ 3. I appreciate direction from leaders, teachers, or elders.
___ 4. I allow others to help me when I am in need.
___ 5. In meditation I am earnest and sincere about strengths and weaknesses.
___ 6. I forgive others who have offended or wronged me.

Courage
___ 7. I know the power of commitment and that fear is weakness.
___ 8. I feel confident that I am loved.
___ 9. I have the courage to help make good things happen in my life or the lives of others.
___ 10. I have the courage to accomplish anything I desire even miracle if necessary.
___ 11. I am confident that I will have a happy successful life.
___ 12. I know that I have the power to achieve goals.

Cleanliness
___ 13. I am clean and orderly.
___ 14. I am dependable and do what I say.
___ 15. I focus on goodness and put unhealthy thoughts out of my mind.
___ 16. I strive to overcome my weaknesses.
___ 17. I feel the influence of a higher power in my life.
___ 18. I believe that planning and order are the keys to success.

Obedience
___ 19. When I meditate I ask for strength to resist urges.
___ 20. I willingly obey rules and follow counsel of leaders.
___ 21. I am confident in my understanding of the concept and principles of peace.
___ 22. I try to live the principles of peace and virtue.
___ 23. I keep the required laws to earn the reward.
___ 24. I do not obey out of fear.

Industry
___ 25. I work effectively, even under pressure or close supervision.
___ 26. I focus my efforts on the most important things.
___ 27. I set goals and plan regularly.
___ 28. I work hard until the job is completed.
___ 29. I find joy and satisfaction in my work.
___ 30. I meditate twice a day.

Integrity
___ 31. I try to be honest with everyone even when others don't see me.
___ 32. I believe that personal integrity leads to reduced anxiety.
___ 33. I think about the needs of others daily.
___ 34. I am patient with myself and with others.
___ 35. I try to help others when they are struggling.
___ 36. I believe that my past does not determine my future.

Wisdom
___ 37. I desire to be of assistance to others.
___ 38. I believe that answers come through meditation.
___ 39. I face challenges and afflictions calmly and hopefully.
___ 40. I earnestly seek to understand the truth and find answers to my questions.
___ 41. I receive knowledge and guidance through meditation.
___ 42. I am able to wait for things without getting upset or frustrated.

Gratitude
___ 43. I tell people that I care and appreciate them.
___ 44. I think daily about what others have done for me.
___ 45. I am thankful for my circumstances.
___ 46. I say positive things about other people.
___ 47. I look for the opportunity to serve other people.
___ 48. I am sincerely grateful for the positive impact of others.

Peace
___ 49. I feel peaceful and optimistic about the future.
___ 50. I am kind and patient with others.
___ 51. I find joy in others achievements.
___ 52. My greatest desire is to be to be peace with myself, neighbors and environment.
___ 53. I love and cherish principles of peace and virtue.
___ 54. I have no desire to be mean, but to be kind to all.

Chapter 2
Why children?

There can be no keener revelation of a society's soul than the way it treats its children.
Nelson Mandela (1918 -)

- *Each of us, regardless of our current age is a child.*
- *As a byproduct of our birth a family was created.*
- *Family is the most significant element of society.*
- *Deliberate nurturing of youth is the greatest influence in tempering individual behavior.*
- *We must never quit learning, developing, growing.*
- *Virtue based training must be re-established within our hearts to be able to positively influence the rising generation, the children of the Millennial Generation.*

Each of us, regardless of our current age, is a child. We have mothers and fathers, individuals who parent us. Some parents are biological while others are not. As a young child, we learned much from these individuals who worked to create a family for us. Despite our physical growth, intellectual advancement, and emotional maturity, the title of child remains ours by the reality that our birth resulted in the formation of a family.

Family is the most significant element of society. From this unit come the educators, the innovators, and the leaders. Values are forged in family settings, consciously or not. Families are designed to bring happiness to children, to allow them to learn correct principles in a loving atmosphere, and to prepare them for life. Parents have the primary responsibility for the welfare of their children. Ideally the integrity and devotion learned at home results from a loving and safe environment. A plethora of virtues including hard work, honesty, determination, and charity are learned at the feet of those who parent us.

Never in the history of the world has there been a greater time for people to embrace a life of virtue. A life based upon time-proven principles can be easily overshadowed by the clamor and turbulence of schedules and deadlines, of economic worries and stress, and of environmental and equality issues. Virtue-based training must be re-established within our hearts so that we are able to positively influence the rising generation, the children of the Millennial Generation.

The Millennial Generation refers to those individuals born between the mid 70s and the turn of the century. This group is characterized by their familiarity with media and communications, and digital technology. Their children are being assaulted by a world exponentially broader and more demanding than even theirs was. Our technology-fueled shrinking world is confronting these young children with unprecedented complexity demanding tolerance and connectivity. Instead of asking the question, "Where does my country fit into the world economy?" these children will be required to ask, "Where do I, as an individual, fit into the global competition and opportunities of the day?" There is an emerging demand for greater maturity at a much younger age than in any previous era. Building on the shoulders of past generations, today's children posses the capacity to absorb and internalize advanced topics at a much earlier age than ever before.

Example

The desire to improve the next generation is driven primarily for the benefit of their children. As parents, our prime objective is to ensure that children learn from our mistakes while sharing our successes. To accomplish this we must be keenly aware of self. Without a knowledge of personal character flaws, they will be passed on to the next generation. Great minds throughout time have advanced the notion that the behavior of the parents will be visible into the third and fourth generations that follow them. This fourth generation halo effect doesn't just refer to positive behavior, but to negative behavior as well. Constructive nurturing of youth is the greatest influence in tempering individual behavior. In time this has a direct affect on the way they will raise and nurture their own children, and so it goes for generations. My behavior in the home and community, regardless of the magnitude, affects children yet unborn, most of whom I will never meet.

How powerful are our actions within the confines of our homes? Children watching and listening are quick to identify our inconsistencies between spoken word and actual performance. Too often personal agendas interfere. Too often we find ourselves over-correcting rather than praising. In most cases the amount of correction far outweighs the words of encouragement and love. Feelings of rejection interfere with critical feelings of acceptance. Soon after the child enters the teen years, the powerful influence of the peer group surfaces. By definition of this relationship, peers praise and accept. The power of this collective identity can influence and persuade good kids to do bad. At this critical point, the parent's positive feedback must outweigh that of the peers or influence will be relegated to the peers. If we provide our youth with transportation, a few emotional challenges and a negative home life, they will select friends in direct opposition to the values they believe their parents represent.

It seems that we are all responsible to some degree for the health and happiness of humanity's children. Just as our feelings of protection and care came from the relationship built with our parents, so our children's similar feelings are related directly to us. We must extend this influence of unconditional love to all children beginning with those in our immediate family and then moving outward. Start with a smile as you pass a child, and then move towards giving of time and talents in neighborhood and community events. Be a volunteer, make a donation, and get involved in teaching and nurturing the children of the Millennial Generation.

Teaching and Learning

Every moment of our lives, teaching and learning is occurring whether we are aware of it or not. The impact of such teaching and learning is far-reaching and never-ending. Above the entrance of a great edifice where I spent a great deal of my life is an engraving from Proverbs: "In all thy getting, get understanding." Not facts, not possessions, not even knowledge but understanding is what is needed. Possibly this understanding is a composite of all learning, combined with critical experiences that add significance and impact. Understanding becomes our quest. We must never cease learning, never quit acquiring information, and never stop developing. Truly this is a lifelong pursuit of knowledge and experience personalized by examples both good and ill. Most of the facts I learned in college are out of date by now. Procedures have been superseded with the advent of new technology. These devices have enabled today's generation to acquire enlightenment, insights, and perspectives never imagined previously. The quest for knowledge is now not so much a matter of acquisition, but rather the development of process. This is how we gain personal experience.

In life we are confronted with challenges from which we formulate questions. Information is collected and tentative decisions are made. With the advice from loving family and friends, our determinations lead to timely plans and actions. Regardless of the ease or struggle that proceeds, successful execution leads to higher plains, broader vistas, and enlightened perspectives. Greater than the actual outcome is the ability to dialogue with the wisdom of age. Repetition builds confidence in the process, reassurance in the decision, and peace in the outcomes.

When I began college I was under the misunderstanding that my objective was to digest a discrete identifiable quantity of facts. Once obtained,

I would then know all and could share it with the rest of the world. A few degrees later, two things became apparent: one, at least half of what I learned proved to be wrong or obsolete within seven years, and two, I was not digesting a set quantity of facts, but was instead learning how to learn. This became critical when considering the future half-life of my degree-based knowledge that would not sustain me beyond the student loan payoff. Unless I could find a method of collecting more timely data in an ongoing, as-needed manner, I was in trouble. The question became the key. I concluded that the wrong solution to the right question is much better than the right answer to the wrong question. Asking myself the right question led me to search for appropriate and timely information. It is not the end, but the process that appears significant. The things I possess I can easily give you, but what I am you must obtain for yourself. I have spent a great deal of time acquiring information so as to be "knowing." Eventually I made the transition to "getting." I am now just realizing that in reality the challenge of life is in "becoming."

Learning how to learn, the "getting" of understanding, is a process, not an arrival. Knowledge and experience alone fall short, but, when combined, can result in intelligence. To set aside arrogance, and humbly accept life's challenges with optimism is timeless growth and unending maturity. To possess knowledge that our choices are as enlightened as possible provides comfort to us. Never without hardship, this is where true learning transpires. Unimaginable highs flow from inconceivable lows. Valiantly we press forward with calmness, peace, and serenity in spite of momentary obstacles and challenges faced. Teach our children how to learn is our goal.

Safety and Security

One of the greatest gifts we can offer a child is a feeling of security and safety. How we communicate this plays a huge role in the child's development of self worth.

I've been told that the majority of effective communication is non-verbal. In other words my expressions, my tone of voice, my body position, and my movements all convey a profound message of their own.

Information that is read and interpreted by the listener either validates the words spoken, or stands in opposition to them. All words must be confirmed by the body language or else doubt, misunderstanding, and hurt can result. Words, both written and uttered, document the formal message, but they do not validate it. The resulting conflict from radically different messages, both verbal and non-verbal, confuse the process. Just as words with multiple interpretations and varying cultural constrains can confound the communication, non-verbal messages compound the setting even more.

And what about physical touch? How does this affect the communication process? Hurt leads to hit and subsequently to hate. Does tenderness lead to embrace and ensuing love in like manner? The force of touch delivered in anger destroys years of good. More significant than this is the power of a heart-felt hug or reassuring squeeze that reinforces the good of the past.

Why children?
As a child within a family, peace begins with parental example, with appropriate teaching and learning, and through the communication of safety and security. As a Child of Virtue, peace begins with me. We are all responsible to some degree for the health and happiness of humanity's children.

Chapter 3

Why is it so difficult?

Great spirits have always encountered violent opposition from mediocre minds.
Albert Einstein (1879-1955)

- We live in a world of opposites.
- From birth, we are required to make choices.
- Due to the perception of limited resource availability, the introduction of other people creates competition, jealousy, opposition, and hostility.
- We learn the behaviors required to secure wants that soon become self-imposed needs.
- Without advice and training, most of us would remain self absorbed.
- Ego is the protector of personal identity whose purpose is to advance individual wants.
- Delayed gratification allows us to succeed.
- Mastery of thoughts, desires, and deeds leads to peace.

There is a story told of a Native American warrior in the sunset of his days, who is passing on life's truths to his grandson. He begins, "A fight is going on inside of me. It's a terrible fight between two mighty wolves: one with beautiful flowing black fur and the other radiant white." He explains, "The shadowy one is Darkness. He is vanity, wrath, envy, lust, cowardice, greed, gluttony, sloth, and fear. The glowing one is Light. He is humility, courage, cleanliness, obedience, industry, integrity, wisdom, gratitude and peace. Son, you have this same fight raging inside of you. So does everyone who has ever occupied this ground." The boy looked confused, and after a moment, asked, "Which wolf will win, Grandfather?" The old warrior counseled, "The one you feed, son. The one you feed!"

We live in a world of opposites. There appears to be opposition in all things: black and white, good and evil, light and dark, rich and poor, happy and sad, pleasure and pain, self and others. From birth, we are placed in circumstances that require choices as to how we will respond to such opposition. From these varied situations, challenges, and appetites, the developmental theorists claim we form our responses. Behaviorists, on the other hand, suggest that we are programmed to respond to situations, challenges, and opportunities through our natural instincts and our environment. A combination of both theories is probably the most prudent position.

Survival

There is a debate about when life begins. I believe that at some point in the womb, the growing fetus becomes conscious of its surroundings: the warmth, the safety, the predictability. At the moment of birth, however, the infant enters an environment that is hostile, cold, loud, intense, and bright. The excruciating journey from the security of the mother's womb is full of struggle and pain. Arriving naked and confused, this new setting is harsh and demanding in comparison. The pain of birth instantly creates dissonance between one's environment and past peace. The arrival begins with the need for food and reassuring touch. Pain leads to tears, and crying leads to relief. To exist, strong instinctive survival behaviors take over to ensure safety and security. Initial peace at this level is equated to the attainment of food and touch, as well as the avoidance of pain. It is soon learned that tears and noise influence the surroundings. Control of the hostile environment has begun. It doesn't take long to perfect these crude survival skills. As long as there are caring attendants near to communicate with, the newborn begins to sense confidence and pride in his/her growing ability to control. This advances to thinking and reasoning, and eventually speech, that is a direct by-product of this struggle. Great effort is expelled in developing this more effective and efficient method of needs gratification. The challenges and struggles involved in learning to speak are overcome by the even greater desire to get serviced quicker and at a higher level. Speech is the most significant development in the pursuit of environmental mastery. As the mind develops and increasingly greater psychomotor skills are acquired, additional desires appear.

Beyond safety and security, satisfaction and pleasure now surface. As the infant's circle of concern expands exponentially, more opportunities present themselves, but alongside this is the notion of competition, as mentioned previously. When other persons are introduced into the infant's world jealousy, enmity, opposition, and hostility follow. This is due to the perception of limited resource availability including competition for food, shelter, safety, security, and attention. "Mine" is a well rehearsed response of this phase of development, and sadly, it is easy to become stuck here.

Once the survival needs are satisfied, we are open to the desire for pleasure. Soon we are seeking out stimulation and avenues of self pleasure and self gratification. When impulses surface we naturally react to them. The more we engage, the greater the desires become. These drives are associated with appetites and passions for food and fun. As with our competitive survival needs, there are similar feelings of rivalry for limited social attention and esteem. Envy, jealously, vanity, and greed lead to anger and wrath when wants and desires are not fulfilled. We soon learn the behaviors required to secure these wants as they quickly become self-imposed needs. As we grow and develop, behaviors become linked or chained together creating patterns of response. Over time these links can grow strong and automatic. The very existence of a routine, even the most disruptive one, provides a degree of stability. Changing these routine behaviors places us in a vulnerable situation that often results in a digression of performance for a while.

Each of us, beginning at infancy, desires a peaceful condition. Our individual approach to the attainment of such a state is as unique as we are. Current beliefs suggest that wealth, position, and power are the most effective sources of peace. By controlling the situation it is assumed that the outcome will be favorable. Great efforts are made to ensure this control. Regardless of the individual realm of influence, it is natural to attempt to gain control over it. Contrary to popular belief, control of others is not the source of peace. In reality, control of self is the key. Peace begins and ends with the individual.

Society

Where two or more individuals exist in a given environment, a society in the loosest form has begun. Personal, professional, and social relationships are the foundation of this society. Such a civilization is based upon mutually agreed upon self-benefiting rules. Basic and often unspoken, these rules define the conditions of membership.

A society carries with it an identity. Members individually determine that it is advantageous to adhere to these rules for their own safety, security, and collective identity. Self centered impulses and desires are controlled through the promise of greater success tomorrow. Once the basic needs of food and shelter are secured, the desire for social interaction, attention, achievement, and attainment arise. All of these are driven by the need to control, and control of self is regulated by the ego. All relationships have a common denominator and this is "you." Each relationship is unique, each is variable, and each is agenda-based. Personal perspective determines each person's reality and without an acknowledgement of individual human weakness and the interdependent nature of the bond, there will be a constant struggle for dominance. This competition for control is the seed of destruction of all unions.

Societies are based upon order and justice. Education and training of the members, and specifically the youth, to the principles and beliefs of the group, is paramount. Parents are the primary teachers. To perpetuate any society, time proven values and ideals must be learned. Trust and obedience to the rules and wisdom of societal elders is initially required until sufficient understanding is secured to ensure adherence to societal truths. By nature we follow the course of least resistance. Without council, support, and direction, most of us will remain self absorbed. As awareness for limited resources is sensed, vanity, greed, envy, and anger surface accordingly. These emotions drive us to advance, achieve, and acquire. The fear of loss develops alongside these attainments. We fear the things we don't understand. Hate is the consequence of fear; we fear things before we hate them. A child who fears the unfamiliar becomes a adult who hates diversity. To regulate these strong emotions, social norms and expectations develop. As these time-proven societal skills are taught to the youth by caring adults and teachers, society and, in turn, the individual should benefit.

Ego

The Latin term for self is ego. We each perform a 24/7 assessment of our lives: every event, act, and competition. We compare where current performances stand with personal perceptions. Innocent at first, within time this process becomes self fulfilling. We see what we choose to see. Numerous ego defense mechanisms are employed to maintain this personal illusion. Ego is not based on the reality of what others witness, but, rather on what we have chosen to believe.

Operating from a position of vanity, envy, greed, and gluttony, the ego is often unaware of the significance others play in personal success. The ego is the protector of self esteem and its purpose is to preserve and advance the individual, and so acknowledging the success of others is counter-productive. Confidence comes from competence in measurable skill attainment. Self-esteem is developed from personal opinions and emotions based upon the feedback of others. Because it is emotionally based, self-esteem is variable and unpredictable. The ego regulates self-esteem. Logic and healthy feedback generate confidence.

So where do pride and humility factor into this passion play of life? Many are born into circumstances which foster humility, if not demand it. Others' situations establish and perpetuate pride. There is nothing wrong with either, and they are not mutually exclusive. Extreme pride or vanity is unhealthy as is false humility or hypocrisy; both can be debilitating.

Success generates self-confidence and pride. The degree of success we enjoy is defined by our ego. Too little pride leads to weakness, discouragement, and depression. Excessive pride leads to vanity, dominance, and cruelty. Excessive ego-driven pride denies the existence of others, as well as the need for assistance from others. Healthy proper pride is born from competence and is what sustains us and supports us in times of difficulty. It also motivates us to succeed and excel. Triggered by fear, unhealthy pride is vanity, arrogance, dominance, and cruelty.

Alongside pride is humility. In today's complex society, competition is the source of additional challenges to humility because of the nature of winning versus losing. Humility, like pride, is a variable condition. Excessive humility is often perceived as weakness and this assumption can lead to discouragement. Conversely, lack of humility leads to unguarded pride and arrogance. Humility is the great regulator of pride. Humility is a healthy acceptance of personal strengths and weaknesses. It is an awareness of the significance of others in the successes of life. Healthy humility leads to forgiveness and service. As such, humility is in direct competition with the ego that wants to dominate others. Establishing and maintaining a balance between humility and pride is no small task, but this is what is needed to master the ego. Achievements and accomplishments naturally lead to confidence and pride. Coupled with healthy humility, healthy pride leads to the motivation to improve self, and to aid in the advancement of others. Identifying this dynamic relationship between pride and humility, assessing our personal condition, and learning to regulate it is indeed the pursuit of life.

Competition

Born self-centered and self-absorbed, we all react either consciously or unconsciously, to the need for survival and the desire for personal gratification. As stated earlier, from the moment of birth impulses surface as environmental situations are presented to us that challenge our very existence. Soon conscious thoughts, plans, and actions are formulated as we pursue the need for nourishment and the desire for stimulation. All this is natural and to be expected. The primal level of survival concerns itself with self preservation and stimulation. Left completely unchecked, most of us will become self-serving, gluttonous, and lazy.

As other people are introduced into our world, competition surfaces, which compounds the initial drives. This is due to a perceived struggle for limited resources. This competition results in greed, anger, envy, and vanity. The fight for food, shelter, security, and attention leads to powerful motivating forces within us to succeed, to control, and to dominate.

What do I choose to do about my ego? Do I choose to manage it or to reward it? Do I choose to control it or empower it? Do I bridle it or unleash it? Few of us, if any, choose to do the latter, but how many of us are willing to pay the price to actively control it? How many of us choose to sacrifice present pleasure for delayed peace? Do I choose to make these choices by formal well-thought-out resolutions, or to just leave them to chance, hoping that things will all work out for the best? By remaining unresolved and uncommitted, options become merely wishes, hopes, and dreams rarely to be realized, especially when consumed by comparison and competition.

Self esteem, pride, and vanity are the byproducts of comparison, competition, and success. Excessive pride and vanity leads to dominance and cruelty toward the competitor. Self control is about regulating these impulses and emotions. Self-discipline is a predetermined choice to delay gratification for the reward of a happier, more secure, successful tomorrow. Delayed gratification requires pre-planning and courage to resist the impulses, urges, lusts, and desires of the moment. The longer these urges have dominated our thoughts the more ingrained they have become. Their pattern of behavior is strong, and the challenge in regulating them is great. Courage is holding to a plan with conviction when everything in the moment is in opposition to it. The pushing and pulling to the course of least resistance generates fear. Fear is self-imposed, and works directly against courage and the pre-determined plan.

History shows that a healthy, orderly society is safer and more secure than the predator/prey world of "survival of the fittest." History also shows that rules protect us as they are the foundation of learning to delay personal gratification. Delayed gratification allows us all to succeed in the orderly, rule-bound social world in which we live. History also shows that education and hard work lead to happy lives. The more advanced the society, the greater the potential for achievement. Rules in any society always have consequences either immediate or in the future. "Getting away with it" is, at best, short term.

Peace is felt in the complete lack of fear and strife. It is a clear conscience free of deceit and dishonesty. Contentment, confidence, and satisfaction are the objectives of us all. Sadly, most of us are confused as to how to attain it. Blindly following impulses has never turned out well for anyone. Peace with others and peace with the environment both stem from peace with self.

The end result of all this discipline and self-control is success. As victory is achieved, it is more than the acclaim of the masses; true personal success is mastery. There is power in knowing that I can master my desires, passions, and emotions. Regardless of the events or circumstances confronted, I remain in control. Others can impose rewards or punishments, support or challenges, but ultimately I determine my actions and reactions. This confidence is a feeling that is indescribable, profoundly desirable, and only attainable through self-mastery. As stated previously, mere success does not ensure peace. Dominance is not peace. Deception is not peace. Manipulation is not peace. Ease is not peace. Hypocrisy is not peace. Fear is not peace. Only when we master ourselves, our thoughts, our desires, and our behaviors can we ever attain the glorious state of peace.

As with any attempt at improvement, failure is a central component. No one hits 100% at first bat. The key to change is to let go of fear. Real growth is learning from failures and setbacks. Failure is only failure when we quit. Until that time, it is feedback, research, and training. Setbacks are only permanent when accepted as fact, and if we quit trying. Here is where personal courage is taken to the test. Getting back up and trying again, and never stopping until it is right, is the action desired. Then and only then are we ready to progress to the next level.

By design we are placing ourselves in an uncomfortable situation. We have to reassess where we fit with this new perspective. It becomes a personal challenge begging for maturity. The mature person will persevere because he will see how the growth will transpire through challenging paradigms.

Why is it so difficult?

Current beliefs suggest that wealth, possessions, and power are the most effective sources of peace. By controlling the situation it is assumed that the outcome will be favorable for us. Great efforts are made to ensure this control. Regardless of the individual realm of influence, it is natural to attempt to gain control over it. Contrary to popular belief, control of others is not the source of peace. In reality, control of self is the key. Peace begins and ends with the individual.

Chapter 4

What is virtuous living?

The shortest and surest way to live with honor in the world is to be in reality what we would appear to be.

Socrates (469BC - 399 BC)

> - *No virtue can be sustained without self control.*
> - *Maturity is control over excess, restraint over impulse, and denial of self.*
> - *Confident personalities come from a life of virtue.*
> - *Virtue training combats the pressures of the vice driven wild.*
> - *Peace is the objective of virtuous living.*

As we become comfortable with the idea of ego and its influence in our behavior, it is reasonable to accept the idea that this ego drives much of our daily concerns, our subconscious thoughts, our reasoning, and, in turn, our behavior. The first step of ego control is recognition. We must identify that strong emotions like fear and desire are dispatched by the ego, and they lead to significant thought and behavior. The management of these extreme emotions is challenging, but the supervision of them is central to getting in touch with who we really are. We must be willing to see ourselves as we truly are, not the image we playfully carry around in our minds. We must see the person that others see. The impressions others have of us are made up from hundreds of interactions, conversations, events, and observations. In our individual quest for a balanced life, the ability to manage, stabilize, and refine humility and pride is paramount in advancing toward personal authenticity and peace.

Authenticity is the degree of reality between the perceived-self and the public-self. The perceived-self is our personal illusion created through selective amnesia, ego fortification, and distorted thinking. This is the image that I have chosen to accept as ME! The public-self is that image that others have of us. It is the observed alignment between word and deed. Inconsistencies are witnessed when performances do not follow verbal pronouncements. The extent of this inconsistency as observed by significant others, combined with our personal acceptance of this perspective, determines our degree of personal authenticity. Low personal authenticity is the result of unhealthy ego dominance. The first step to genuineness is acknowledgement of possible contradictions.

What we are today comes from our thoughts of yesterday, and our present thoughts build our life of tomorrow: our life is a creation of our mind.
Buddha (563 BC – 483 BC)

Individuals administer their own internal rewards and punishments for their personal behavior. Control over responses is imposed upon us to achieve goals, and to adhere to personal and societal standards. No virtue can be sustained in the face of an inability to control oneself. We all possess a random mix of virtues and vices at differing intensities. As such, improvement of any given attribute can only be attained when it is a conscious choice to do so. Without self control, our natural impulses will lead to habits, and for most of us our natural tendencies lean toward vices over virtues. Without conscious self-control, vices will exist with the potential to become a driving force behind personal behavior. A virtue must be accepted, committed to, and practiced before its benefits are seen. Once we are disciplined and in control of personal appetites, emotions, and responses, we are then free to pursue goals and objectives which are determined as being valuable. This control over excess, restraint over impulse, and denial of self is maturity in its highest form.

Again, referring to the 8 Virtues Attributes Assessment at the end of Chapter 1, frequent testing results in increased personal awareness. It's not so important as where you are in the process as it is that you are continually thinking about the virtues and incorporating the resulting behaviors into your life. Like a garden, the mind can be either actively cultivated or ignored and neglected, but either way it will yield growth. We attract and harbor that which we love, as well as that which we fear. Our ego reaches the height of its personal aspirations and then falls to the level of its uncontrolled desires. Each season more seeds are developed and planted by the process of germination. Every seed sown or allowed to remain will take root and will flower in time. The seeds that are allowed to grow are the ones that will dominate. Without conscious selection, weed seeds will reproduce as easily as good seeds. We, as our own gardener, must cultivate our individual ground of thoughts and deeds. When the weeds are removed, the fruits and flowers flourish. Consciously removing the wrong and the useless within our own minds will improve the positive, the useful, and the pure. Continual attentiveness reveals personal flaws with increasing accuracy in thought and understanding. Over time, personal character will blossom and destiny will be determined.

When we lack self-control, base thoughts crystallize into conscious habits that lead us to adverse circumstances. Fear, doubt, and indecision materialize into weak, sub-human, slothful habits that solidify into circumstances of failure. Until thought is linked to purpose there is no intelligent accomplishment. Without a central purpose in life, petty woes, fears, troubles, and self-pity easily consume us. Before we can accomplish anything we must lift our thoughts above animal indulgence.

The attitudes we exhibit within our own unique circumstance is largely a result of choice. The beliefs we hold in our heart will become truth. Those things we admire we will become. However, a small change today can result in dramatically different tomorrows. By following the highest source of light, strong character develops and a life of virtue fosters a confident personality. By rising above base desires and passions, we can ascend to our highest self possible. The point is that we design our lives through the choices we make. Significant individuals will be placed in our path to guide, warn, and protect us, but ultimately we are responsible for the degree of light we display.

Failure to self-regulate is central to all current world problems. Addictions, abuse, violence, war, crime, underachievement, debt, and obesity are at epidemic proportions. In contrast, no negative patterns are associated with personal self-control. Self-regulation functions like a muscle where initial fatigue results in greater strength, and repeated exercise over time develops greater control. It is unclear as to whether self-regulation can be taught; scenarios and conditional statements may help. Is it the nature of the child or the nurturing of the parent that is most responsible for self-regulation? We can demonstrate the process, but ultimately it is the will of the individual that determines replication, practice, and behavior change. Regardless of the motivation behind change, it is clear that virtue training is needed to combat and eradicate the consequences of unrestrained vices. The power of this concept has its greatest applicability to children. Children are young, fresh, and malleable. Building upon these natural virtue/vice associations, we can encourage and reinforce attainment. Like the twisted steel cable, each individual wire in and of itself lacks great strength, but evenly woven together under tension, results in a carrying capacity exponentially greater than the sum of the individual wire. Called synergy, this is a powerful principle of the universe.

Fundamental Construct

Although not a novel idea, the concept of choosing and defining virtues to live by is a worthy endeavor. Many would argue that in today's rapidly changing world, virtues have become lost in the quagmire of fast-paced, sensory-infused, technology-based forms of information which daily assault our minds whether we like it or not. The 8 Virtues presented here are an attempt to re-establish core societal values from which many cultures have evolved since the beginning of time. The continuous improvement cycle begins with Humility, Courage, Cleanliness, Obedience and Industry. Integrity is the turning point allowing further development. Wisdom is the benefit of Integrity development. Gratitude is required to ensure continuation of the process. After the initial cycle a greater awareness of Peace is experienced. Once completed the cycle begins again with renewed Humility. During each subsequent cycle a higher level of virtue is achieved. Individual circumstances are unique to each of us and so is the time required to complete each cycle. This process is not about speed or even completion. It is about lasting personal change.

8 VIRTUES CYCLE

The 8 Virtues which have been identified as the process to achieving personal peace are organized into four fundamental virtue constructs: Core Virtue, Foundational, Virtues Power Virtues, and the Sustaining Virtue. These virtue constructs are represented by the visual of a classical structure.

FUNDAMENTAL CONSTRUCT

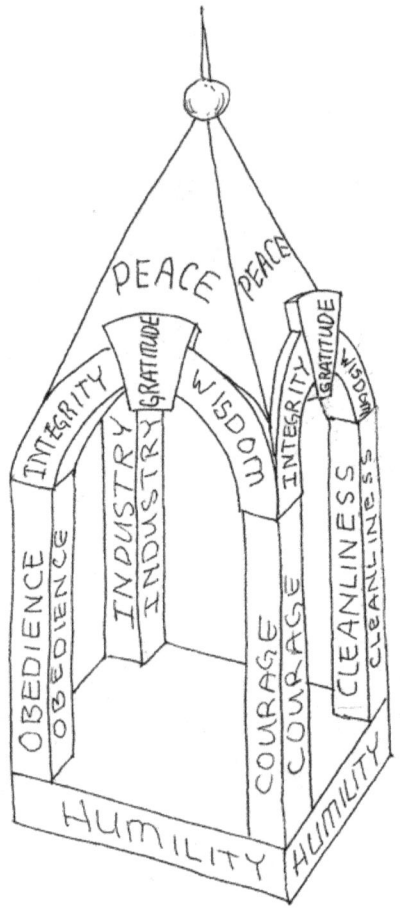

The Core Virtue (Humility) is followed by four Foundational Virtues (Courage, Cleanliness, Obedience, Industry). Two Power Virtues (Integrity, Wisdom) lead to the Sustaining Virtue (Gratitude) with the subsequent reward of the process being Peace.

The Core Virtue is the bedrock footing upon which the Foundational Virtues are positioned. The structure is only as good as its foundation. As discussed in Chapter 1, these foundational virtues of Courage, Cleanliness, Obedience and Industry result in success. These skills of success are transient without a genuine core base.

Built upon a solid footing of Humility, the structure is sound and resistant to the storms of life. If the Foundational virtues of success are erected on common ground, the resulting structure becomes unstable at best. Without this ordered, planned Core footing of Humility, chaos is inevitable.

CHAOS

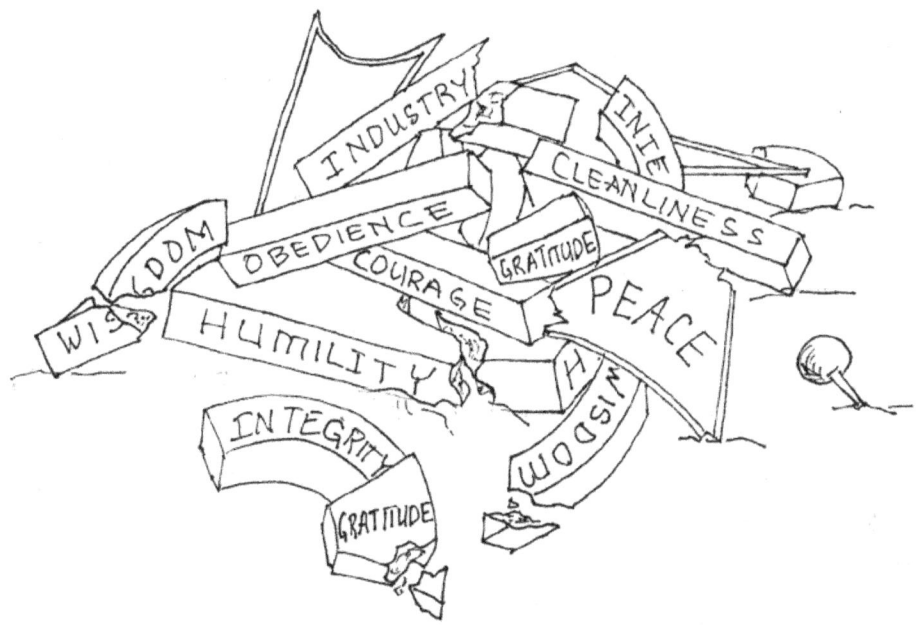

The Power Virtues of Integrity and Wisdom provide the strength to the arch. They can become utilized only after the preceding footing and foundational attributes are functional. It is the Sustaining Virtue of Gratitude which is the final stone that is placed in the structure that ensures continuous improvement, progression, and ultimate strength. As the last stone placed in the arch, the keystone, its significance is vital. In the actual creation of an arch, stones are laid in unison ending with this hand-fitted stone which accounts for any flaws in the columns. Resting upon this well-designed and constructed configuration is the roof. Vital for safety and security, the roof of Peace provides the ultimate protection from the elements and other intrusions. The roof, or capstone, is only as good as the structure supporting it.

What is virtuous living?

Without conscious self control, vices will exist with the potential to become a driving force behin personal behavior. A virtue must be accepted, committed to, and practiced before its benefits are seen. We must be willing to see ourselves as we truly are. We must see the person that others see. Virtuous living is authentic living.

Chapter 5

How does it work?

We cannot change our thoughts without changing our lives in the process.
James Allen (1864 - 1912)

> *The 8 Virtues are:*
> - *Hierarchical in structure,*
> - *Interconnected with pivotal moments determining virtue attainment,*
> - *Cyclical in nature requiring delayed gratification for progression,*
> - *Targeted for children and young people,*
> - *Educationally sound with meaningful and measurable objectives.*

Virtues have existed in one form or another for centuries. They are not culturally bound; all great civilizations throughout time have recognized the need to live by guiding principles. Virtues are universal standards and by definition imply self control. The difference between other value development efforts and the 8 Virtues presented here lies in the following five defining characteristics: hierarchical structure, interconnection, cyclical nature, target audience, and academic presentation.

Hierarchical Structure

In the ideal world these virtues are rank ordered and hierarchical, but in reality they often display themselves randomly under a variety of conditions. This is because we are not only comprised of unique, individual natures but in our youth we were also nurtured in the development of specific traits. Good or bad, each of these virtues or vices are part of who we are. Approaching development and change in a logical, consistent manner maximizes growth and so we have emphasized the consistent, not the exception, in our presentation here.

This program is based upon an initial core virtue with each additional virtue building upon the previous ones. All are interconnected and synergistic, with the whole being greater than the sum of the individual parts. As with any goal or objective, delayed gratification is the key to attainment.

- The Core Virtue is Humility because without this we limit our personal peace. Humility has a huge impact upon our level of teach-ability.
- Courage, Cleanliness, Obedience and Industry are the Foundational Virtues of success, and competence in them is required before the Power Virtues of Integrity and Wisdom can be achieved.
- The capstone of the process is the Sustaining Virtue of Gratitude. Gratitude strengthens Humility and ensures that the Power Virtues will remain and grow. It also perpetuates the cyclical nature of the entire process as Gratitude becomes critical in sustaining each virtue at each level.
- The ultimate goal is the attainment of Peace, achieved only after mastering and internalizing the 8 Virtues.

Interconnection

The 8 Virtues are interconnected as they work together to create a virtuous and peaceful life. This is only achieved when individuals make predetermined choices to acquire virtues over vices. This pivotal moment of choice is influenced by personal perspective or bias toward the virtue or the vice. At many points in all of our lives, decisions are made to live a virtuous life or not. The following table identifies observed behaviors indicating personal bias at pivotal moments in the virtue/vice contest.

Pivotal Moments Table

Personal Bias	Virtue or Vice	Observed Behaviour
ATTITUDE	• Humility • Vanity	Forgiveness Blame
COMMITMENT	• Courage • Cowardice	Strength Fear
ORDER	• Cleanliness • Lust	Planning and organizing Chaos
FAIRNESS	• Obedience • Gluttony	Adherence to justice & rules Consumption to dullness
WORK	• Industry • Sloth	Organized success Apathy and indifference
HONESTY	• Integrity • Greed	Personal ethics "Getting" at all costs
REASONING	• Wisdom • Envy	Methodical deliberation Impulsive reactions
COMMUNICATION	• Gratitude • Wrath	Thanks to all and for all Anger towards all

The ego drives humility and vanity. The pivotal moment in the humility and vanity association involves personal attitudes towards other people. We each must truthfully answer the question of how important others are to us. The degree of acknowledgment we have for other people in general is critical to virtuous living. This is validated by the extent of acceptance or rejection of responsibility for the relationships we have created with others, as witnessed by our actions and personal behaviors. Vanity is self-absorption resulting in a lower degree of the service one is willing to offer to another. Humility is honest recognition of self, resulting in an increased level of responsibility and liability one is willing to accept for the relationship created. Forgiveness is demonstrated acceptance of relationship responsibility. Personal levels of humility and pride vacillate between people-centered and self-centered perspectives. Sadly, by default of personal weakness, the void will most always be filled with self.

Commitment is the key to courage over cowardice. The key variable underlying courage is personal resolution or commitment. The decision to be courageous occurs prior to the challenge. Either by training or through a predetermined personal vow, when confronted with challenges or obstacles, fear and vulnerability must be neutralized for courage to surface. Left unchecked, the instantaneous reaction is flight. Courage is a social behavior. Acts of courage are relationship-based and involve other people. Reflecting back on the humility and pride discussions, the pivotal moment regarding commitment is directly affected by the degree of recognition we have for others. This is followed by the degree of acceptance of responsibility a person has for the relationships created with others. Courage is people-centered requiring self-sacrifice, whereas cowardice is self-centered and pain avoidant.

Order is the common denominator between cleanliness and lust. Cleanliness is based upon order and planning, whereas lust is unregulated, self-absorbed chaos. Cleanliness is related to personal health and hygiene, living environment, and moral refinement. Without order in any of these areas, anarchy will prevail. Without order, disease and desire are left to run rampant. Reflecting back on the humility and pride discussions, the pivotal moment regarding order is directly affected by the degree of recognition that we have for others. This is followed by the degree of acceptance of responsibility a person has for the relationships created with others. As part of this personal quest for enlightenment, the goal is to order our lives so as to become people-centered as opposed to self-centered.

At the pivotal moment, our bias towards fairness is the determiner between obedience and gluttony. Obedience provides the power for fairness and justice. Justice is the societal system based upon rules that promise personal protection of rights and freedoms. Obedience is the price paid for this personal insurance. Obedience involves delaying the nearby compensation for a later, greater return. Obedience at the social level is protection, rewards, and punishment avoidance. Gluttony is immediate gratification; it is over-consumption to the point of waste. It is void of all rules and fairness. Justice doesn't apply to the self-absorbed glutton. Gluttony affects everything from availability of goods and services, to disregard and disdain for the needy. Reflecting back on the humility and pride discussions, the pivotal moment regarding fairness is directly affected by the degree of recognition that we have for others. This is followed by the degree of acceptance of responsibility a person has for the relationships created with others. Obedience is people-centered, whereas gluttony is self-centered.

The difference between an industrious person and a slothful one is personal vision and individual level of commitment to work for that vision. Plans lead to productivity resulting in rewards from others. Plans begin with goals, and they involve time management. Operating in a self-absorbed vacuum, driven solely by personal gratification, there is no need for acceptance, accomplishment, achievement, or productivity. Lazy or slothful behaviors are self-absorbing and self-reinforcing, resulting in ever greater sloth. Reflecting back on the humility and pride discussions, the pivotal moment regarding work is directly affected by the degree of recognition that we have for others. This is followed by the degree of acceptance of responsibility a person has for the relationships created with others. Industry is people-centered, whereas sloth and laziness is self-centered.

Personal honesty is the foundation of integrity, but not of greed. Integrity is about truthfulness to self and to others. It is uniformity between thoughts, words, and deeds, and it reflects personal ethics. Greed is covetousness to the point of obsession. It's about manipulation, dishonesty, and deception. Greed is getting, at all costs. Such getting includes manipulating the truth, and stealing for personal gain. True integrity is not simple to identify because it is based upon private motives. Reflecting back on the humility and pride discussions, the pivotal moment regarding honesty is directly affected by the degree of recognition that we have for others. This is followed by the degree of acceptance of responsibility a person has for the relationships created with others. Integrity is people-centered, whereas greed is self-obsession.

The personal honesty associated with integrity frees us from the mental conflict associated with competing ideas. This freedom opens the mind to pursue loftier ideals. Mature reasoning leads to wisdom, while unchecked emotions lead to envy. Wise people control extreme emotions that enable rational thought. The conflict between wisdom and envy begins with the emotional cancer of comparison. When we engage in comparing individual contentment against the situation and circumstance of others, envy is the outcome. The very definition of envy is discontentment. Envious people are only as satisfied as their ability to acquire the next greatest thing. Direct comparison to others means that we are never content. Wisdom is the lack of envy. Wise people appreciate where they are in life, and what they have. This level of contentment opens them up to a sense of gratitude. Wise people desire things for their intrinsic worth, not their social power. Reflecting back on the humility and pride discussions, the pivotal moment regarding reasoning is directly affected by the degree of recognition that we have for others. This is followed by the degree of acceptance of responsibility a person has for the relationships created with others. Wisdom is people-centered, whereas envy is self-centered.

It is a personal choice whether I prefer to communicate gratitude or wrath. What is the difference between the most sincere prayer of thanksgiving and the most heated of verbal tongue-lashings? How about the gentlest act of kindness as opposed to the cruelest act of brutality? Both are extreme, one with words and the other with behaviors. Both are driven from deep-seated emotion. Both are passionate, high-energy communications. Both radically affect those on the receiving end of the conversation. Reflecting back on the humility and pride discussions, the pivotal moment regarding communication is directly affected by the degree of recognition that we have for others. This is followed by the degree of acceptance of responsibility a person has for the relationships created with others. It becomes a matter of being people-centered and expressing gratitude openly, as opposed to being self-centered and allowing unregulated thoughts, anger, and rage to engulf everyone. It is an issue of allowing positive or negative energy to dominate, and it is witnessed through communication to others.

Cyclical Nature

The 8 Virtues program is cyclical in nature. The upward bound virtue spiral begins with the desire to live in peace. It is a conscious choice to delay the gratification of the moment and commit to strive, to reach, and to sacrifice for the greater reward of peace. Aside from the many pivotal moments associated with the individual virtues, there is a distinct point when each of us makes the decision to pursue virtue or to allow vice to prevail. Consciously, or through unregulated impulse response and the subsequent default choices that follow, our actual behavior reveals our true perspective.

ORDER

PEACE

FEAR

Either way, these virtues or vices are incorporated into our lives, and once the cycle has begun, it is extremely difficult to alter. Just as the pull of gravity must be overcome to attain space flight, so it goes with the peace progression. One must be vigilantly committed to the benefits of delayed gratification to prevail in virtuous living. It is a constant struggle, but there is a point where gravity's hold is broken. Little effort is required at the orbital level of space flight, but unfortunately, there is a natural momentum in the downward spiral. As with gravity, the vice spiral possesses the inborn drive of immediate self-gratification. The pull is relentless and self-fueling. The yearnings can never be fully satisfied so one is trapped in a cycle of unfulfilled passion. Just as the 8 Virtues cycle progressively higher, the opposing vices cycle lower. It is just as continuous as the virtue cycle, but rather than a goal of improvement, it cycles to degradation, self-absorption, and a state of constant fear. Regardless of the rationalizations and excuses made, we alone make the choice of which cycle to engage in, either by default or by conscious decision. If not a conscious choice, decision by default will prevail.

CHAOS

PEACE

OBEDIENCE INTEGRITY GRATITUDE
APATHY WISDOM WRATH COWARDICE COURAGE
CLEANLINESS VANITY LUST GLUTTONY HUMILITY
GREED SLOTH
INDUSTRY

FEAR

Without order and planning, chaos results. This extreme level of meaninglessness is the characteristic response to ever-increasing stimulus where eventually our ability to cope completely depletes due to the sheer intensity of the impulses. This creates a state of emotional chaos consisting of disorder, confusion, and complete unpredictably as depicted in the graphic above. There is an overwhelming feeling that "everything is out of control." As with the soldier who has survived the bombings, the machine guns, the dead, and the maimed, a sense of disconnected numbness and complete indifference to normal activities overtakes the mind, body, and soul.

Current life patterns have evolved over time in each of us. These routines, healthy or damaging, protect us and can give us a sense of stability. The Attributes Assessment, introduced in chapter 1, provides invaluable personal insight if we choose to use it. It is significant to note that these various routines also enslave us and become the greatest obstacles for change. It is important that virtue patterns be established in children as early as possible so as to resist the downward draw.

Target Audience

The target audience for 8 Virtues training is children and young people. Today's technology-fueled shrinking world is confronting children with unprecedented, ever-changing complexity, and the demand for tolerance and connectivity. Today's youth have a greater capacity to grasp advanced topics and vocabulary at a young age due to information availability. They possess the capacity to understand and internalize many of the foundational principles upon which strong families and powerful societies are built. The SamiTales Program is a timely idea to aid in the stability of the world by providing an unwavering foundation for this audience of eager minds. Such a firm foundation will enable children everywhere to adapt, adjust, and flourish in this ever-changing, increasingly complicated, and demanding world. The primary audience of this program is preschool, home school, and K-6 children of all cultures. In the process of instructing children it is understood that adults will also refresh and internalize the virtues as they teach them.

Academic Presentation

The vision of the SamiTales Program is to enhance children's sensitivity, skills, and understanding in order to enable them to adapt to the demands of, and to thrive in our changing world. By capturing and sustaining a child's attention, we can educate them. Research indicates the economic, social, and personal value of investing in the lives of children in a positive and constructive manner avoids the social and penal system costs that may later result. To meet this need, the 8 Virtues Series offers a curriculum as discussed in Chapter 2 that serves as a personal core value system for participants.

Assembled upon the thoughts and practices of diverse philosophers and developmental theorists, this program seeks to identify, clarify, and magnify various global standards of character-building qualities that can assist children in coping with their changing world. Children will delight in the stories and curriculum offered. Objectives are clear and measurable.

Each storybook is based upon the life experiences of Sami Seamonster. Modeling is used as the teaching tool. The characters indirectly model positive and negative examples of the virtues. Conclusions are drawn with wisdom and advice transferring from the adult characters to Sami and his friends.

Repetition and visual symbols representing each virtue guarantees easy recognition and recall. Key to the 8 Virtues Program is the crest.

CREST

The motto, "Child of Virtue, Peace is My Purpose," is located at the bottom of the crest as a reminder of the mission of this work. The crest shows how the virtues build upon one another, with the end goal of attaining peace. Gratitude is the central symbol emphasizing that all other virtues are sustained by it. The crowning achievement is the star which sits atop the crest to signify the peak attainment of peace. Supporting the star is the 8 Virtues rainbow. Each of the virtues is represented by a distinct color symbolically displayed in the rainbow.

How does it work?
The 8 Virtues program enables children and young people to attain individual authenticity in their quest for personal peace through:

> *hierarchical structure,*
>
> *interconnection,*
>
> *cyclical nature,*
>
> *storybook presentation for children, and*
>
> *educationally sound curriculum.*

	Virtue	Definition	Color	Symbol		Motto
1	Humility	Humility is a healthy balance between strengths and weaknesses.	Pink		Key	Humility is modestly and meekly moving towards mercy and service to others.
2	Courage	Courage is commitment to facing fears and challenges	Red		Heart	When courage is discharged, fear is conquered.
3	Cleanliness	Cleanliness is order of body, space and mind that leads to planned health and happiness.	Green		Leaf	Cleanliness removes clutter and confusion, and creates space for contemplation and consideration.
4	Obedience	Obedience is compliance through respect and performance.	White		Scales	Obedience requires patience and resilience, performance and respect
5	Industry	Industry includes setting goals, managing time, working hard, and being persistent.	Orange		Gears	Work will work, when wishy washy whining won't.
6	Integrity	Integrity is honesty to self resulting in consistency between thoughts and actions.	Blue		Arrow	Integrity is the capacity to show accountability with sincerity.
7	Wisdom	Wisdom is earned through knowledge and experience.	Purple		Crown	Words of wisdom grow as we reflect on the truths we know.
8	Gratitude	Gratitude is expressing thanks for all things.	Tan		Hand	The platitude of gratitude is the attitude of thanks.
9	PEACE	A state of bliss, happiness, serenity, and calmness; absence of fear.	Yellow		Star	Peace is my purpose.

Chapter 6

What is the CORE Virtue?

> - *Humility is the CORE virtue.*
> - *Pivotal moments in humility and vanity involve personal attitudes towards other people.*
> - *Humility requires us to think of our abilities as no greater and no lesser than they really are.*
> - *Humility is healthy acceptance of personal strengths and weaknesses.*
> - *Mastery of humility releases stored energy that drives one through the 8 Virtues to the attainment of peace.*

The <u>Core Virtue</u> is **Humility**. The core of anything is the center. As with the earth, a baseball or a golf ball, the dense resilient inner core stores the potential/kinetic energy which, when released, propels the ball forward. Humility is the core virtue. Mastery of this virtue releases the stored energy that drives one through the succeeding virtues leading to the crowning achievement of Peace. Without this solid footing, the foundational virtues of success may be fleeting and temporal, rarely facilitating peace. The deep solid nature of Humility provides the energy and thrust necessary to propel one forward beyond self interest.

HUMILITY Core Virtue

**Humility is nothing but truth,
and pride is nothing but lying.**
Vincent de Paul (1581-1660)

Humility and vanity are all about individual attitude, which is influenced by our ego. A decision is made to develop a forgiving heart by accepting liability for conflict, or to engage in blaming. The pivotal moment in the humility and vanity association involves personal attitudes towards other people. Individually each of us must truthfully answer the question, "How important are other people to me?" The degree of recognition we have for other people in general is the critical awareness we seek. This is validated by the extent of acceptance or rejection of responsibility for the relationships created with other people, as witnessed by action and personal behavior. Pride is self-absorption resulting in a lower degree of service one is willing to offer to others. Humility is honest recognition of self resulting in an increased level of responsibility and liability that we are willing to accept for the relationships created. Forgiveness is demonstrated acceptance of relationship responsibility. Personal levels of humility and pride vacillate between people-centered and self-centered perspectives.

Humility is the healthy acceptance of personal strengths and weaknesses. It is a state of self-awareness, and the acceptance of situations, conditions, and circumstances. It is based upon the degree of acceptance of personal liability for a given incident or set of circumstances. At one extreme is blame, which is a rejection of all responsibility, and at the other extreme is forgiveness, which demonstrates ownership of the current condition. Generally, concerning relationships, forgiveness is associated with a failing, a flaw, an insult, or an incident resulting in misunderstanding, hurt, and offense. Forgiveness is showing response control when wronged, misunderstood, persecuted, betrayed, offended, or victimized. Blame, on the other hand, is an effort to accept no ownership for the current situation. It is the personal perspective of pointing the finger, or rationalizing, justifying, and denying behavior. Lies, fabrication, deceit, hypocrisy, and fraud arise out of this non-acceptance of personal liability.

Positive reinforcement will encourage humility. It includes accurate feedback, giving service, seeking forgiveness, and developing close relationships. The goal is to enable the child to feel safe and secure enough to non-defensively acknowledge personal strengths and weaknesses. Honest motives are required to succeed with this type of virtue training. Attaining proper humility will not come if motivated solely by a parent or some other source. One must be personally committed to the goal of inner peace and the prudent life.

By nature we are self-centered, prideful, and prone to carnal appetites and passions. In order to regulate these appetites and passions, a change of nature is required. This is attained through training and self-discipline. Often it is a byproduct of the humbling process where, through a series of challenging circumstances or trials, we come to see ourselves as human and imperfect. Humility simply requires us to think of our abilities and our actions as no greater, and no lesser, than they really are. True humility requires that each of us become acutely aware of ourselves: our strengths and our weaknesses. It demands an honest appraisal of ourselves. When such a sincere assessment occurs, pride diminishes. Greater humility fosters greater forgiveness, which in turn leads to lingering humility. Humility oftentimes conjures up images of weakness, submissiveness, and fear, but this is a false idea. True humility is strength, confidence, and courage.

In our competitive, demanding world it is easy to believe that vanity and pride are positive qualities. They are touted as the measure of a healthy self esteem, and a way to succeed in life. Feelings of confidence and contentment are important to succeed in life's goals. Full-blown, in-your-face pride gets out of control because it is based on the emotional cancer of comparison and competition. Each person's pride is in competition with everyone else's pride. By nature, it is aggressive and destructive. Pride gets no pleasure out of having something, only out of having more of it than the next person. We say that people are proud because they are rich, or clever, or good-looking, but vain people are only happy by being more rich, or more clever, or better looking than someone else. If everyone became equally rich, or equally clever, or equally good-looking, there would be nothing to be proud about. It is the comparison that makes us proud; it is the pleasure we feel by being above someone else. Once the element of comparison and competition are gone, pride also diminishes, but, unfortunately, proper humility is not always what takes its place.

Humility can be easily confused with false modesty. I think we've all been guilty of false modesty at one time or another. This occurs when we are recognized for an accomplishment and we act as though it really wasn't that important or significant. Sometimes we devalue what we've accomplished under the pretense of humility, but it becomes false humility because in actuality we are seeking for more praise and adulation from others.

The question surfaces, then, how is humility practiced? The simplest answer is to give credit where credit is due. Do you take as much credit for a success as possible, or do you seek to shine the spotlight on others and acknowledge the strokes of luck that came together to make things successful? No one ever succeeds on the strength of his/her own merits alone. Always along the path of success there are supportive family members, friends, teachers, and coaches or mentors. Humble people show restraint when promoting personal strengths. They understand that others have equally important and interesting successes to share. Humble people go about doing what is expected without making a big deal about it. If the skills of success are built firmly on the footing of humility, peace will naturally grow. Without proper humility, fear will instead stimulate greed, envy, and wrath.

The humility progression is additive, developmental and expansive:

    1.   <u>Humble Acknowledgement</u>. The first level of humility is

exhibited by a personal willingness to risk time, effort, and emotion to understand personal strengths and weaknesses. The very act of introspection allows for the possibility of infallibility and limitation. This self-inspection is only as valid as the attitude of the observer. Self-esteem is generated through self-respect.

2. <u>Humble Validation</u>. The validation of personal strengths and weaknesses comes through open, honest self-assessment. This leads to a personal commitment to overcome one's limitations by internalizing the virtues. The desire to refine self can generate greater personal-esteem if maintained in a healthy perspective.

3. <u>Humble Forgiveness</u>. Forgiveness is central to true humility and self-control. Forgiveness is proactively showing response control when wronged, misunderstood, persecuted, betrayed, offended, or victimized. Forgiveness can be personal or relational. When one openly offers forgiveness to another, visible behavior is observed that leads to external acknowledgement of internal thoughts.

Humility MOTTO:
"Humility is the capacity to show accountability with sincerity."

Mark each statement:

1 never, 2 occasionally, 3 often, 4 frequently, 5 always

_____ *I am meek and forgiving.*

_____ *I accept constructive feedback from others.*

_____ *I appreciate direction from leaders, teachers, or elders.*

_____ *I allow others to help me when I am in need.*

_____ *In meditation, I am earnest and sincere about strengths and weaknesses.*

_____ *I forgive others who have offended or wronged me.*

> ## What is the CORE virtue?
> Humility is the core virtue. Without this solid footing, the foundational virtues of success are fleeting and temporal, rarely facilitating peace.

Chapter 7

What are the FOUNDATIONAL Virtues?

> - *The FOUNDATIONAL virtues are the four steps to success.*
> - *Courage is bravery, fortitude, strength, valor, and gallantry.*
> - *Cleanliness is about planning and order.*
> - *Obedience is the virtue that promotes justice.*
> - *Industry is the capacity of being engaged in a cause.*

The <u>Foundational Virtues</u> are the four steps to success. They are **Courage, Cleanliness, Obedience** and **Industry**. They provide the stability, consistency, and reliability for growth and development. As the base underpinnings, these four virtues, as with the cornerstones of a building, are crucial in the erection of stable walls and a strong roof. These Foundational Virtues lead to success in any endeavor undertaken. They also become the cornerstones on which the Power Virtues are built. The byproduct of success is pride, but when these four virtues rest soundly on the core footing of Humility, pride and vanity are managed and Peace is possible. They provide the support and stability needed as we advance toward greater self-control of thoughts and actions.

COURAGE Foundational Virtue

From where the sun now stands, I will fight no more.
Chief Joseph (1840-1904)

The difference between courage and cowardice is all about commitment. A decision is made prior to the event to be strong and proactive in the face of adversity. The fundamental moment underlying courage is this personal resolve. The choice to be courageous occurs prior to the challenge. Either by training or through a pre-determined personal pledge, when confronted with challenges or obstacles, fear and vulnerability must be neutralized. Left unchecked, the immediate reaction is flight. Courage is a social behavior that comes from facing fears and challenges. Cowardice, on the other hand, is a lack of robustness or internal strength when challenged with danger or dread. Cowardice is weakness of character due to a non-committed nature. Without principles, values, or a moral code, cowardly people are unable to resist opposition. Acts of courage are relationship based and involve other people. Reflecting back on the humility and pride discussions, the pivotal moment regarding commitment is directly affected by the degree of recognition a person has for other people. This is followed by the degree of acceptance of responsibility that a person has for the relationships created with others. Courage is delayed gratification at it's finest. Courage is people-centered which requires self sacrifice, whereas cowardice is self-centered and pain avoidant.

Courage is bravery, fortitude, strength, valor, and gallantry. When challenged, three types of courage emerge: physical, emotional, and moral. Physical courage is the ability to confront fear and pain, as well as to risk uncertainty in the face of hardship or threat of death. Emotional courage deals directly with fear and the imaginings of the mind. Moral courage is the ability to act appropriately in the face of temptation, opposition, shame, scandal, or discouragement. Courage is derived from love: love of something or someone beyond self. It originates in the mind.

> **You cannot run away from weakness;**
> **you must sometime fight it out or perish;**
> **and if that be so, why not now, and where you stand?**
> *Robert Louis Stevenson (1850-1894)*

The act of "taking a stand" is by nature uncomfortable and threatening, but courage flows from the drive to stand up to something that is deemed unjust, evil, or against the value system. The greater the physical opposition, however, the easier it is to convince the mind that it is unwise to take a stand. Regardless of the source of the opposition, it is the mind that determines the need to take a stand. As the contest of wills escalates, the risk also exponentially increases. The stakes become high and the determination to hold to original beliefs is challenged again and again until one position either folds or advances. Courage can be exerted towards self, as well as towards others. These are threats and challenges to safety and life, threats and challenges to pride and reputation, and threats and challenges to beliefs, values, and esteem.

One isn't necessarily born courageous, but we are all born with potential. We can practice courage. It is the motivation to take risks, the strength to be compassionate, and the wisdom to be humble. Courage is the foundation of integrity. It is not simply one of the virtues, but it is the strength behind every virtue at its testing point. Mark Twain said it well: "Courage is resistance to fear, mastery of fear, but not absence of fear."

Cowardice asks the question, "Is it safe?" Expediency asks the question, "Is it politically correct?" Vanity asks the question, "Is it popular?" But, integrity asks the question, "Is it right?" There comes a time when one must take a position that is neither safe, politically correct, nor popular, but we take it because our conscience tells us that it is right. Martin Luther King, Jr. stated: "The ultimate measure of a man is not where he stands in moments of comfort and convenience, but where he stands at times of challenge and controversy."

Becoming a more courageous person will require us to dig deep within and find the will to achieve our goal, and to commit to overcoming any barriers that enter into our path. To increase in courage the following steps are important:

1. Pre-determine responses for specific situations. Create mental scenarios and determine ahead of time how to act when faced with challenges. By establishing and practicing ethical responses before they are faced, we empower ourselves to resist the easy path in the heat of the moment.
2. Write down daily goals that are manageable and measurable so you can focus on the task to be accomplished. Knowing exactly what is to be accomplished maintains motivation as well as resolve, in the heat of the moment.
3. Be patient and flexible. It is easy to lose our resolve when we experience setbacks but we must remember that diversions often occur when the wrong strategy is being used. Albert Einstein stated, "Insanity is doing the same thing over and over again and expecting different results."
4. Be confident. Keep the vision. Never doubt what can be accomplished. Rise above setbacks and failures by learning from them.

Courage comes in three varieties: physical, emotional, and moral. In the courage progression they build upon each other as opposed to replacing one another. Additionally, each can be at different phases or stages. Physical courage is the most base, tangible, and readily confronted. Emotional courage deals directly with fear, and the intangible imaginings of the mind. Moral courage addresses the ethical dilemmas of the ages.

The courage progression includes:

1. <u>Physical Courage</u>. When humankind is confronted with tangible threats to life, freedom, or wellbeing, physical courage is required to face the danger. These threats include objects, persons, and organizations that challenge personal safety, peace, and security. This type of courage requires a muscu-

lar body, strong heart, and quick mind. Physical courage is outwardly observable, and self-esteem is developed through victory and self control.

2. <u>Emotional Courage</u>. Fear is very real to the fearful. Grown from imagination, paranoia, or insecurity, to the fearful, these foes are genuine, and to the degree they have been allowed to dominate have or may become all encompassing. Taken to the extreme, we can become powerless through fears and phobias. Conquering inner fears requires mastery of emotions. Inwardly measurable self-esteem flows as mastery is attained.

3. <u>Moral Courage</u>. This level of courage includes the ability to manage the dilemmas we face between perceived right and wrong. Tied to personal ethics and subsequent integrity, these inner battles between the moral and the dreadful, between exactness and dishonesty, between truthfulness and rationalizations are real, deceiving, and ethically deadly. Distortions, manipulations, and exploitations all move reality around subtlety and slowly, deceiving even oneself if not constantly vigilant.

Courage MOTTO:
"When courage is discharged, fear is conquered."

Mark each statement:

1 never, 2 occasionally, 3 often, 4 frequently, 5 always

_____ *I know the power of commitment and that fear is weakness.*

_____ *I feel confident that I am loved.*

_____ *I have the courage to help make good things happen in my life or the lives of others.*

_____ *I have the courage to accomplish anything I desire.*

_____ *I am confident that I will have a happy successful life.*

_____ *I know that I have the power to achieve goals.*

CLEANLINESS Foundational Virtue

**Better keep yourself clean and bright;
you are the window through which you must see the world.**
George Bernard Shaw (1856-1950)

Cleanliness is about planning and order. A decision is made to sacrifice time and effort to live an organized, orderly life. Without such a decision we allow impulses, desires, and yearnings to control us. Cleanliness is based upon orderliness leading to planned health and happiness, whereas lust is unmanaged, self-absorbed chaos. Planning leads to productivity resulting in rewards from others. Plans begin with setting goals, managing time, and being persistent. Without such plans we operate in a self-absorbed vacuum driven solely by personal gratification where there is no need for acceptance, accomplishment, achievement, or productivity. Cleanliness is related to personal health and hygiene, individual living environment, and private moral refinement. Without order in any of these areas, there is physical and emotional pandemonium. Without order, disease and desire are left to spread like an epidemic. Self-indulgent devotion to personal gratification, lust, and yearning places everything and everyone else as secondary. When lustful earthly passions and unrestrained impulses dominate our thoughts to the point of obsession, the door to addiction is opened. Reflecting back on the humility and pride discussions, the pivotal moment regarding order is directly affected by the degree of recognition that we have for other people. This is followed by the degree of acceptance of responsibility a person has for the relationships created with others. As part of this personal quest for enlightenment, the goal is to order our lives so as to become people-centered as opposed to self-centered.

The familiar Christian proverb, "Cleanliness is next to Godliness," has never been more applicable in today's fact-paced, multifaceted, uncertain world. It is interesting to note that other world faiths and prominent figures also promote the necessity of cleanliness for overall well-being. Sri Sathya Sai Baba, a spiritual leader from India, noted that "a person might be an expert in any field of knowledge or a master of many material skills and accomplishments, but without inner cleanliness his brain is a desert waste." Krishna, the deity worshipped across many traditions in Hinduism, insists on outer cleanliness and inner cleansing. Gandhi believed that "conversion without cleanliness of heart can only be a matter of sorrow, not joy, to a godly person." From the Koran, the central religious text of Islam, it states, "God loveth the clean." The 19th century German philosopher, Friedrich Nietzsche noted that "what separates two people most profoundly is a different sense and degree of cleanliness."

Cleanliness, then, is of mind and body, thought, and action. The mind is the source of all behavior. Deep within the folds of the brain are established beliefs that drive our every action. Impulses become thoughts, and thoughts become plans. Plans are eventually acted upon, and over time these actions become habitual behaviors which can lead to addictions. The benefits of a clean body, environment, and mind are improved health and wellness, positive image, beauty, and order. All of these lead to purity of thought and action. A healthy body, through nutritious food, exercise, good hygiene and habits, leads to a healthy mind that is the foundation of order. The healthier the mind the better the choices we make, all leading to even greater opportunities. Just like the environment where we determine the frequency and depth of the housecleaning, we must also organize our mind and throw out the unwanted trash. Replace the nonsense with positive thoughts and plans that will lead to positive actions and deeds. A healthy mind comes from a vigorous body and environment, and a healthy body develops a dynamic mind.

By focusing upon the health of the body and mind as a foundational virtue, the recipient's capability for mastery is maximized. Children must be taught order, and to be clean in all aspects of their lives. Order, as opposed to clutter, should be emphasized. Sloppy housekeeping leads to sloppy habits. Sloppy habits lead to sloppy nutrition. Sloppy nutrition leads to sloppy health, and sloppy health leads to sloppy performance. Dirty homes lead to unhealthy bodies and weak minds.

Taking pride in cleanliness and order develops one's attention to detail, improves personal work ethics as well as self-confidence. Moreover, cleanliness facilitates the orderly development of one's life. Let all your things have their place; let each part of your business have its time. Benjamin Franklin understood that if he wanted to get important things done in his life, he had to make sure the little things wouldn't get in the way. People strive to order their lives so that they can have peace and tranquility. Cleanliness keeps our mind clear and our life organized. When the house is a disaster, our thinking is going to feel similarly disorganized. Feng Shui, an ancient Chinese system of aesthetics using the laws of heaven and earth to improve surroundings, suggests there is a natural connection between the order of the environment and the state of our mind. Clutter will overwhelm and result in stress whereas a clean, well-organized environment lifts our spirits.

How we present ourselves in life is paramount, and cleanliness creates a positive image. Messy, unkempt clothing and homes result in judgments about our character and personality. Unfair, possibly but it's just how the world works. When we present an orderly and clean appearance to others, they will assume that all aspects of our life are in accordance.

Cleanliness leads to beauty. That which is neat, well proportioned, and symmetrical appeals to the eye and creates beauty. As we transform our lives to be orderly and clean, we increase the amount of beauty in our lives. By living the preceding virtues of humility and courage, one's mind, body, and moral fiber are strong enough to ensure that valuable and available effort and time be filled with positive adventures and projects.

The effect of cleanliness extends beyond the body and the environment to our character. Virtue cannot dwell long in filth, and moderation in thought is the window through which we see the world. By keeping our thoughts clean and bright, our actions and behaviors will likewise reflect fresh, unsoiled clarity and transparency. We must live with ourselves and thus it is in our best interest to be the best company possible.

Cleanliness is a natural progression from personal hygiene, to surroundings, to thoughts and feelings. The cleanliness scale is additive and progressive. As lower aspects are ordered it opens the opportunity for the next level of purity. Clean bodies are healthy bodies. Clean homes house unpolluted minds. Clean minds foster vigorous thoughts.

The cleanliness progression includes:
1. <u>Clean Body</u>. The body requires order and planning as does any complex machine. Low-level thinking germinates in dark, dirty places dressed in filth and decay. To clean the mind, first clean the body. Pride and self-esteem have a direct correlation to health and hygiene.
2. <u>Clean Environment</u>. The body requires sanitary surroundings to remain healthy. The mind requires an orderly environment to function clearly. To organize the mind, organize the home. Pride and self-esteem have a direct correlation to living environment and atmosphere.
3. <u>Clean Mind</u>. The body requires maintenance, interaction, and nutrition in order to function properly. The mind reflects its surroundings: trapped in chaos, the mind loses discipline; isolated, the mind loses perspective; starved, the mind loses accuracy. To energize the mind first energize the body. To organize the mind first organize your surroundings. Plan to be organized.

Cleanliness MOTTO:

"Cleanliness removes clutter and confusion, and creates space for contemplation and consideration."

Mark each statement:
1 never, 2 occasionally, 3 often, 4 frequently, 5 always

_____ *I am clean and orderly.*

_____ *I am dependable and do what I say.*

_____ *I focus on goodness and put unhealthy thoughts out of my mind.*

_____ *I strive to overcome my weaknesses.*

_____ *I feel influence of a higher power in my life.*

_____ *I believe that planning and order are the keys to success.*

OBEDIENCE Foundational Virtue

**Each day look into your conscience and amend
your faults; if you fail in this duty you will be untrue
to the knowledge and reason that are within you.
Keep a watchful eye over yourself as if you were your
own enemy; for you cannot learn to govern yourself
unless you first learn to govern your own passions and
obey the dictates of your conscience.**
Kahlil Gibran (1883-1931)

Obedience and its attendant vice of gluttony are both about fairness. A decision is made to be either fair in all your affairs, or to disregard the needs of others and consume everything to excess. Obedience provides the power or impetus to receive justice. Justice is a societal, rule-based system that promises fairness in the personal protection of rights and possessions. Obedience is the price paid for this personal insurance. It involves delaying an immediate reward for a later greater reward. In contrast, gluttony is immediate gratification; it is over-consumption to the point of waste. It is void of all rules and fairness. Justice doesn't apply to the self-absorbed glutton. Gluttony affects everything from availability of goods and services to a conscious disregard for the needy. Reflecting back on the humility and pride discussions, the pivotal moment regarding fairness is directly affected by the degree of recognition that we have for other people. This is followed by the degree of acceptance of responsibility a person has for the relationships created with others. Obedience is people-centered, whereas gluttony is self-centered.

Obedience is the act of carrying out commands. Obedience is honesty to society. At this basic level, we either obey to avoid punishment, or to gain a reward. Regardless of our personal motive, compliance to the rules is voluntary. Obedience is given to figures of authority, such as children to elders, students to teachers, citizens to government, and humanity to a Higher Power. Learning to obey adult rules is a major component of socialization in childhood. Uninformed rebellion is anarchy. Beginning with fear of punishment, obedience eventually evolves to higher levels of societal good.

As we age, our level of obedience matures and becomes more refined. Many lament that they would have made less errors in judgment if they only knew at a young age what they have gained in old age. The curiosity and arrogance of youth eventually withers, and age-old truths emerge as significant. The very writing of this text is a direct example of this process within me. This justice naturally resides within our hearts, but over-rebellious, non-conforming desires resist it. We all want justice, safety, and protection, and obedience is the premium which we pay for it. Anne Sullivan, instructor of Helen Keller, noted, "I have thought about it a great deal, and the more I think, the more certain I am that obedience is the gateway through which knowledge, yes and love, too, enter the mind of a child."

In the past, absolute obedience was expected and even demanded from children. Today it seems we expect everything of children except obedience. In an effort to sustain personal agency, many parents of today are content to let the child make personal choices regardless of their capacity and understanding in such judgments. A balance is needed where the child begins by making small, insignificant choices with accompanying consequences, both positive and negative. Mother Teresa believed that strength lies in being obedient in small things. From here we gain the experience and wisdom to make larger and more significant choices.

Aristotle believed that the ordering of society is centered in justice. Obedience is the virtue that promotes justice. It is achieved when respect is given and duties are performed. Failure to obey leads to self absorption and gluttony. This vice of over-indulgence and over-consumption of anything and everything represents unfair distribution. Historically, the eating of delicacies and costly foods was considered gluttony. Today, gluttony not only refers to excessive eating and drinking, but also to any and all unrestrained behaviors that extend beyond what is good for one's health and well-being.

Have you ever noticed that the first few bites of delicious food are the best? After eating something for a while the vibrant tastes become significantly dulled. Today many people shovel food into their mouths so fast that their palate does not have a chance to register the sweet, the sour, or the spice. When the stomach is full it tries to tell us that it's time to stop eating but, unfortunately, people ignore this signal and continue to eat far past capacity. The consequence is not only a far less enjoyable eating experience, but also an ever enlarging midsection.

Currently, the developed nations of the world have a consumption factor of 32, while the rest of the developing worlds' 5.5 billion people consume at a rate closer to 1. This means that one billion people consume 32 times more than 5.5 billion others. Unsustainable consumption by the gluttonous is exceeding personal capacity, as well as robbing others of minimally meeting basic needs due to resource depletion and poverty resulting in the reduced personal health of all. Gluttony in the modern world, due to affluence and lack of consideration for others, has enabled a ruling class to exist. This group of self-serving individuals is distinguished by a spirit of entitlement, and they display lust, egotism, greed, and obesity.

Beginning with the fear of punishment obedience can evolve to higher orders of behavior and motivation. Obedience through social commitment is the next level of performance. These ethical levels progressively increase personal integrity as one works to arrive at absolute fairness.

The obedience progression includes:
1. <u>Fear of Punishment</u>. The first level of performance is visible to others. Physical actions and behavior are observable and thus quantifiable by the outside world. Because performance is measurable, social pressures become a great motivator. Like obeying a traffic law, the fear of being punished or of receiving a reward enforces compliance. Self-esteem is enhanced and monitored by the opinions of others.
2. <u>Social Contract</u>. The second level of performance is invisible to others. Motivation is emotionally based and subjective. Here we obey the law because it is right, and because it

maintains the social order. Whether my actions are seen or not, I follow my own internal set of beliefs for my own reasons. Self-esteem is enhanced/monitored from within self.

3. <u>Absolute Justice</u>. The third level of performance is invisible because it transcends the individual. Motivation is spiritually based and independent of even the person's direct benefit. Obedience to the law is offered because it is right and just. One is motivated from impressions and beliefs which reach beyond personal gain. Self-esteem is enhanced and monitored from a Higher Source.

Obedience MOTTO:

"Obedience requires patience and resilience, performance and respect."

Mark each statement:

1 never, 2 occasionally, 3 often, 4 frequently, 5 always

_____ When I mediate I ask for strength to resist urges.

_____ I willingly obey rules and follow counsel of leaders.

_____ I am confident in my understanding of the concept and principals of peace.

_____ I try to live the principles of peace and virtue.

_____ I keep the required laws to earn he reward.

_____ I do not obey out of fear.

INDUSTRY Foundational Virtue

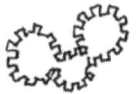

**Be not afraid of going slowly;
be afraid only of standing still.**
Chinese Proverb

Industry and sloth are both about our perspective towards work. A decision is made to take charge of your life, create a personal vision, and commit to success, or to accept no ownership for your future. The difference between industrious persons and slothful ones is the vision they hold, and their experience with work. Lazy or slothful behaviors are self-absorbing and self-reinforcing, and eventually result in apathy. Sloth follows a path marked by listlessness, melancholy, lack of joy, depression, indifference, despair, hopelessness, and despondency. We slip into sloth by following the course of least resistance, or by neglecting to take proper care of something in a timely manner. Reflecting back on the humility and pride discussions, the pivotal moment regarding work is directly affected by the degree of recognition a person has for other people. This is followed by the degree of acceptance of responsibility that person has for the relationships created with others. Industry is people-centered, whereas sloth and laziness are self-centered.

Industry is the capacity of being actively engaged in a cause. Efficient and effective people always possess the ability to manage their time in order to accomplish more. By living the preceding virtues of humility, courage, cleanliness and obedience, one's mind, body and moral fiber are strong enough to ensure that valuable and available effort and time are filled with positive adventures and projects. Industrious people lose no time in making and achieving worthwhile goals. Time management is essential, as well as consistent and persistent effort. Self-respect is developed from receiving an honest grade for an honest effort, or honest pay for an honest day's labor. Time is a gift that needs to be filled with positive acts and deeds. Making every hour of one's existence count is the goal of being industrious. Industry suggests that temporarily living with discomfort is acceptable because you are engaged in something worthwhile, something important, and something that lives beyond self.

Idleness robs us of proper pride and the joy of success. Idleness is depression's playground. Depression is real and has the capability of consuming positive thoughts and energy. To avoid depression we need to be industrious by planning our days, focusing on worthy goals, finding a passion that is beyond self, eliminating distractions and noise, and looking for opportunities to engage with others.

The preliminary focus of most people appears to be service to self. Service to others is a conscious choice that must be made. Can leisure activities have any meaning in the absence of work? Often we feel overworked and can't wait for a holiday. When it finally arrives, a peculiar thing happens: the first days of relaxation are fantastic, the next couple of days are enjoyable, but after that it gets boring and meaningless. Too much time empty of purpose dulls our senses. We start to feel anxious and once more want to be engaged in doing something useful.

Work encourages individual responsibility. Personally choosing to do things rather than delegating tasks to others results in ownership of the task at hand. A sense of accomplishment is earned, and self-respect is gained. We all have gifts and talents that should be shared with others; we all have something to contribute in making our family, community, and world a better place. What we choose to do with our gift of time demonstrates where our hearts are. The challenge is to fulfill our true potential and to make every hour of existence count. John Witherspoon, a signatory of the United States Declaration of Independence, said, "Do not live useless and die contemptible."

Being industrious counters feelings of sadness, melancholy, and despair. Idleness invites self-absorption and discouragement. By nature we want to feel useful, to make and provide things for others, and to be engaged in causes greater than ourselves. Work provides a reason to get up each day. It provides a sense of accomplishment. It enables us to leave a legacy that will outlive us.

To become industrious we must plan to be. Third President of the United States, Thomas Jefferson, said "It's amazing how much you can get done if you're always doing." Before going to bed, prepare for the next day by organizing and prioritizing necessary tasks. One reason people flounder around and waste time during the day is because they don't know what they should be doing. This can be avoided by scheduling the day out. Find a system that works for your unique and individual needs. Some people like to schedule every minute of the day, while others just like to have a list of tasks that need to be completed. Some people like online or digital planners, while others like paper based planning systems. Personally, I use a scrap of paper where I list my tasks for the day. I then quickly rank order them by importance and then schedule them, allowing enough space on the paper for notes. Folding this neatly I stuff it in my pocket and refer to it throughout the day to see if I am on task.

Industrious people accomplish worthy goals. It's natural to spend time focused on what you have determined to be important. By committing to admirable goals, either through verbal pledge or in writing, we will make ourselves and the world around us better. We become what we spend our time at. With every moment of our lives a time investment decision is made. Stop and ask yourself, "Will this action bring me closer to my goal?" If not, don't do it.

Time is the great equalizer in life. All of us regardless of age, gender, nationality, or creed have been given exactly the same hours in a day, exactly the same minutes in an hour, and exactly the same seconds in a minute. Most of us allow this precious commodity to dwindle away a few moments at a time because we just never take the time to control it. The goal is to keep our lives focused, effective, and efficient while also keeping in mind the need for productive leisure and recreation. Shouldn't we pursue activities that will make us better people? True recreation is an activity that leaves us energized and ready to take on difficult or mundane tasks. The idea is to stay busy, but at a relaxed pace.

Industry is planning and action. It can be viewed on a progressive, additive scale. The industry progression begins with service to self. This is the initial focus of all people. Service to significant others is the next logical path to work towards as one labors to become industrious. Eventually industrious individuals will arrive at universal service to all humanity. As the external rewards of industry are lessened in this progression, the connection to the entity being served increases.

The industry progression includes:
1. <u>Service to Self</u>. Being actively engaged in a self-serving cause is better than no industry at all. Efficiently satisfying personal needs and agenda is easily observed by all. Measurable performance is the key here. Self-esteem is derived from accomplishment, achievement, and attainment.
2. <u>Service to Loved Ones</u>. Once personal needs and wants are satisfied one's attention can then turn to significant others in need. Great acts of sacrifice have been recorded to family and friends requiring support. Occasionally such acts are unrecognized, but most often they are acknowledged. Self-esteem is immediate and forthcoming in abundance, and love for those being served increases dramatically.
3. <u>Anonymous Service</u>. The highest level of industry is when we are anxiously engaged in a good cause towards individuals unknown to us. Such service includes invisible acts of kindness willingly and freely given where personal recognition is avoided, and anonymity is maintained. This type of service transcends the individual, and rewards are from a Higher Source. Self-esteem is self generating and contagious. Love for humanity grows in breadth and depth.

Industry MOTTO:

"Work will work when wishy washy whining won't."

Mark each statement:

1 never, 2 occasionally, 3 often, 4 frequently, 5 always

_____ I work effectively, even when I'm not under pressure or close supervision.

_____ I focus my efforts on the most important things.

_____ I set goals and plan regularly.

_____ I work hard until the job is completed.

_____ I find joy and satisfaction in my work.

What are the FOUNDATIONAL virtues?

The FOUNDATIONAL virtues are:

Courage, Cleanliness, Obedience, and Industry. They provide stability, consistency, and reliability for growth and development. Together they lead to success in any endeavor undertaken.

Chapter 8

What are the POWER Virtues?

- *The POWER virtues are Integrity and Wisdom.*
- *Integrity is a deep seated value of rightness, of consistency of thought, of principles and of deed resulting in the absence of cognitive dissonance.*
- *Wisdom is a gift earned through virtue development. It grows in the fertile ground of the clear conscious.*

The <u>Power Virtues</u> are Integrity and Wisdom. They will only develop if grounded on the core virtue of Humility, and resting safely on the Foundational Virtues of Courage, Cleanliness, Obedience, and Industry. The degree of mastery of each of these skills is directly related to the ultimate peace that is attainable. The Power Virtues are cyclical and progressive, and as with any skill, practice enhances improvement. The development of these Power Virtues is witnessed as one advances toward greater self-control in thought and deed. As mentioned in Chapter 1, Integrity is the pivotal factor in determining the ultimate outcome. More than societal honesty, Integrity is personal honesty leading to a clear conscience which allows for undistracted reasoning that opens the door to Peace.

INTEGRITY Power Virtue

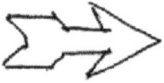

Live that so when your children think of fairness and integrity they think of you.
H. Jackson Brown, Jr.

Integrity and greed are both about honesty. A decision is made to be honest in all dealings by adhering to personal ethics, or to disregard truth, and then dishonestly move to acquire anything and everything, regardless of the cost. Integrity is about truthfulness to self and others. It is consistency between thoughts, words, and deeds. Greed is covetousness to the point of obsession. It's about manipulation, dishonesty, and deception. Greed is "getting" at all costs, including lying, stealing, deceit, and distortion for personal gain. True integrity is not easy to determine because it is based upon personal motives. Reflecting back on the humility and pride discussions, the pivotal moment regarding honesty is directly affected by the degree of recognition a person has for other people. This is followed by the degree of acceptance of responsibility that person has for the relationships created with others. Integrity is people-centered, whereas greed is self-centered to the point of obsession.

Integrity is a deep-seated value of rightness. It is consistency of knowledge, actions, values, methods, measures, thoughts, and principles. Integrity is often regarded as the quality of having an intuitive sense of ethics and truthfulness. Integrity begins in the mind and soul, and for this reason it is difficult to measure because personal motives can rarely be validated. So many of our true motivations are, at best, unseen or left to self-report. The political "spin" is the enemy of integrity. In the political arena, meaning and motive are as difficult to pin down as it is to stick jell-o to a wall or move mud up a hill. Integrity is consistency of character combined with a committed refusal to engage in behavior that evades responsibility. Integrity is freedom from deceit, hypocrisy, or duplicity. It is honesty in intention. At the heart of integrity is truthfulness in all conduct and all communications. Honesty and integrity are the marks of greatness. People with integrity seek to be sincere in all communications by becoming a person who keeps confidences, curbs sarcasm, and avoids dishonesty.

Integrity is understanding what is right, ethical, or best, and then acting appropriately upon that knowledge. Conversely, greed is understanding what is right or best, but then acting on a desire to possess more than one needs or deserves. It is an unbalanced desire to possess wealth, status, power, or goods. Greed is coveting what others have or are. It is a strong drive for excess attention, possessions, status, acclaim, and so on. Greed, like all vices, can dominate earthly thoughts. Greed is identified by disloyalty, deliberate betrayal, treason, hoarding, trickery, exploitation, violence, and corruption, all for personal gain.

Another form of integrity is showing respect for information. When we share information about another person with others, we have no idea where it will end up. Like a bag of feathers thrown into the wind, it is impossible to ever account for each one. Most of us would never dream of robbing a bank or stealing friends' possessions, but many of us are far less careful with an equally valuable piece of property: private information. No matter how the information came, the sacredness of information possessed should be closely guarded. Integrity begs us to be such a person of honor. Gossip can hurt both the gossiper and the person being discussed. The gossiper loses respect because mistrust is validated by the very action of gossip, which is inherently dishonest. Even innocent or inaccurate allegations leave permanent damage.

Integrity is the ethics of the entire 8 Virtues system. Being engaged in all the right performances for all the wrong reasons is vane. Integrity is the act of taking personal responsibility for actions and decisions. Actions and behavior can be measured, but the effort of the internal struggle cannot be. By living the preceding virtues of courage, cleanliness, obedience and industry, success is achieved, and pride is gained. Once attained, additional efforts result in abundance. Erected upon a foundation of humility, one's mind, body, and moral fiber are strong enough to ensure that valuable and available effort and time be filled with positive adventures and projects.

Integrity means being true to ourselves. It means being honest, upright, and decent in our everyday dealings with others. Our actual conduct speaks for us more eloquently than words ever could. Integrity becomes the basis for both reputation and self-respect. If we can't be honest with ourselves, we won't be honest with others. It requires self-awareness, since we cannot accurately communicate what we don't know. People of integrity can be counted on to stand up for what is right, even if it is unpopular, and to behave with honor even when there is no one around to see. Integrity allows other people to trust us because they know that we value our commitments and seek to live by them. J.C. Watts, who became one of the first children to attend an integrated elementary school in the U.S., stated, "Character is doing the right thing when nobody's looking. There are too many people who think that the only thing that's right is to get by, and the only thing that's wrong is to get caught."

Cognitive dissonance, as mentioned earlier, is the mental discomfort experienced from conflicting ideas being present at the same time. The degree of integrity one achieves is in direct inverse proportion to the degree of mental dissonance experienced. As integrity grows anxiety diminishes, allowing mature reasoning to increase. Integrity, therefore, sets the stage for increased wisdom and the attendant virtues of gratitude and peace.

The growth of personal integrity is additive and progressive. The integrity progression begins with visible acts of consistency between word and deed. When there is consistency between thoughts and unseen acts, a second level is attained. At the third level there is little regard to the outside opinions of others. Behavior is independent and transient to personal gain.

The integrity progression includes:

1. <u>Integrity is Visible</u>. Physical actions and behavior are seen and quantifiable to the outside world. Because behavior is measurable, social pressures become great motivators to ensure consistency with the declared word. Self-esteem is monitored and enhanced by the opinions of others.

2. <u>Integrity is Invisible</u>. Physical actions are still monitored but the personal intent now becomes the object for consistency validation. This motivator is hidden to the outside world. Only after reflection and candid review can truth be revealed. Whether actions are seen or not, personal ethics are adhered to. Self-esteem is enhanced and monitored from within.
3. <u>Integrity Transcends the Individual</u>. The personal legacy of behavior outlives the individual. All actions and efforts are directed to others. Service and sacrifice are the prime motivators. Individual comfort and gain is, at best, secondary. Driven by a higher goal, behavior is consistent and enlightening. The needs of the "other" are paramount to all actions. Self-esteem is a by-product of higher living.

Integrity MOTTO:
"Integrity is the capacity to show accountability with sincerity."

Mark each statement:

1 never, 2 occasionally, 3 often, 4 frequently, 5 always

_____ *I try to be honest with everyone even when others don't see.*

_____ *I believe that personal integrity leads to reduced anxiety.*

_____ *I think about the needs of others daily.*

_____ *I am patient with myself and others.*

_____ *I try to help others when they are struggling.*

_____ *I believe that my past does not determine my future.*

WISDOM Power Virtue

**They live in wisdom who see themselves
in all and all in them.**
Bhagavad-Gita

Wisdom and envy are both about thinking and reasoning. A decision is made to engage in methodical deliberations, or to succumb to impulsive reactions. The fundamental issue between these two opposing behaviors deals with the emotional cancer of comparison. The act of comparing personal contentment against the situation and circumstances of others is vanity, and envy is the outcome. The very definition of envy is discontentment. Envious people are only as satisfied as their ability to acquire the next greatest thing. Direct comparison to others means they are never content, as in this context, contentment becomes a moving target. Wisdom is the lack of envy. Wise people appreciate who they are, where they are, and what they have. This level of contentment opens them up to a sense of gratitude. Wise people desire things for their intrinsic worth, not their social power. Wise people control extreme emotions, and this allows rational thought to surface. Reflecting back on the humility and pride discussions, the pivotal moment regarding reasoning is directly affected by the degree of recognition a person has for other people. This is followed by the degree of acceptance of responsibility a person has for the relationships created with others. Wisdom is people-centered, whereas envy is self-centered.

Wisdom is not a trait that is achieved, but rather a gift that is earned through the knowledge and experience gained while progressing through the preceding virtues. Wisdom flourishes in the mind of the honest soul. Freed from the anxiety associated with cognitive dissonance and the guilt associated with conflicting thought, wisdom grows. Integrity removes inconsistency and incongruity allowing wisdom to flourish. Wisdom is a thinking pattern developed after disciplined practice and personal evaluation and experience. It is a deep understanding of the complex interactions of people, things, events, and situations, resulting in the individual ability to consistently choose or act in such a way as to produce optimum results. Wisdom demands emotional control gained through delayed gratification in order to minimize personal opinion and preference so that time-proven principles, knowledge, and insights can prevail. The comprehension of what is true or right gets coupled with the best possible judgment as to what action to take.

A fleeting virtue, wisdom must not be taken for granted. It must be nurtured and sustained in order to grow. As one's wisdom increases, close acquaintances will witness the benefits of improved decision making on major visible issues. Over time, a personal sense of rightness develops, and flourishes. Eventually, purposeful reflection will attend even the most minor or seemingly insignificant choices in one's life. The end result of advanced wisdom is the right to direct perception or insight received from great minds of the past and present, as well as a Higher Power. Wisdom is knowing the appropriate time to act, and the appropriate words to speak. By living the preceding virtues of humility, courage, cleanliness, obedience, industry, and integrity, one's mind, body, and moral fiber are strong enough to ensure that valuable and available effort and time be filled with positive adventures and projects.

> **How much better it is to get wisdom than gold!
> and to get understanding rather than silver!**
> *-Proverbs*

Wisdom is achieved when envy is controlled. Resentments are created from the inability to conquer the ego's insatiable desire to have and possess another person's good fortune, success, qualities, possessions, or happiness. It is the sentiment that another person has something perceived as lacking in oneself. It is a desire to deprive other people of their belongings, wealth, relationships, status, and so on. It includes thoughtless, reckless, and self-absorbed thinking that leads to hatred and cruelty. Experience, knowledge, and reason lead to wisdom; this is the true aim of teaching. It is the capacity to realize what is of value in life. Beyond simply knowing and understanding the options available, wisdom provides the ability to differentiate between them, followed by the power to choose the best alternative.

Envy and jealousy are often used interchangeably, but in reality these words represent two distinct emotions. Envy is associated with pain or frustration that is caused by another person having something that we do not personally possess, such as beauty, wealth, or status. Jealousy is the fear of losing to another person something that we possess. Jealousy typically refers to the negative thoughts and feelings of insecurity, fear, and anxiety over an anticipated loss of something that the person values, such as a relationship, friendship, or love. It consists of a combination of emotions including anger, sadness and disgust. Envy and jealousy result from different situations and are distinct emotional experiences, but both exist when one gets pleasure from the misfortunes of others. A child can feel jealous of her parents' attention to a sibling, and envious of a neighbor's new bike. Envy and jealousy are equally potent causes of unhappiness.

Aristotle defined envy as "the pain caused by the good fortune of others." Eighteenth century German philosopher, Immanuel Kant defined it as "a reluctance to see our own well-being overshadowed by another's because the standard we use to see how well off we are is not the intrinsic worth of our own well-being but how it compares with that of others." He went on to say "If science is organized knowledge, then wisdom is organized life." Plato, echoing this sentiment, took it a step further: "It's better to be wise and not seem so than to seem wise and not be so; yet men for the most part desire the contrary."

The expression of wisdom is a gradual progression to enlightenment. The first level of this wisdom progression begins with conscious, methodical deliberation over major decisions. As one progresses to the next level, reflection and care is given in all decisions, including seemingly minor or inconsequential ones. The final level of wisdom is achieved when direction and inspiration from a higher source is perceived. This personal revelation is identifiable and acknowledged.

The wisdom progression includes:

    1. <u>Wisdom in Major Decisions</u>. Methodical deliberation over major decisions and events is engaged in. This is a conscious effort. It is a deliberate break from past behavior

where impulsive reactions and choices were the norm. Significant others take note of the change, as decisions become healthier and outcomes better. Praise and support is offered openly, which in turn enhances esteem.

2. <u>Wisdom in All Decisions</u>. Increased reflection and care are given to all decisions regardless of their magnitude or significance. One's life begins to change for the better with regard to personal health, finances, and social position. The rewards of sound thinking are witnessed personally, as well as by close acquaintances. A calmness, safety, and security follow such provident living, and self-esteem is enhanced accordingly.

3. <u>Wisdom in Life Management</u>. At this level wisdom is received in the form of inspiration. Although indirectly observable, the individual is the true monitor of this influx of insight and creativity. As the mind is awakened and the understanding quickened, even common things seem new. These fresh insights begin to flood the mind as the impact of personal choice is seen in its true light. Actions are driven by lofty motives as the perspective moves from self to service. Sacrifice becomes part of the daily vocabulary as purpose takes on a deeper, broader meaning driven by greater good.

Wisdom MOTTO:

"Words of wisdom grow as we reflect upon the truths we know."

Mark each statement:

1 never, 2 occasionally, 3 often, 4 frequently, 5 always

_____ *I desire to be of assistance to others.*

_____ *I believe that answers come through meditation.*

_____ *I face challenges and afflictions calmly and hopefully.*

_____ *I earnestly seek to understand the truth and find answers to my questions.*

_____ *I receive knowledge and guidance through meditation.*

_____ *I am able to wait for things without getting upset or frustrated.*

What are the POWER virtues?

The Power virtues are Wisdom and Integrity. People of integrity behave with honor even when there is no one around to see. People of integrity can be counted on to stand up for what is right even if it is unpopular. Being free from mental conflict allows for wise thought. Wise people appreciate who they are and what they have.

Chapter 9

What is the SUSTAINING Virtue?

- *The SUSTAINING virtue is Gratitude.*
- *Maintaining a thankful attitude improves psychological, emotional, and physical well being.*
- *Feelings of gratitude lead to more energy, increased optimism, better social connections, and greater happiness.*
- *Gratitude is the power behind wisdom and peace.*
- *Gratitude sustains all the virtues ensuring that they will not diminish.*
- *Gratitude is expressing thanks for all circumstances.*

The Sustaining Virtue is **Gratitude**. It is the keystone of the edifice, and maintains the delicate state of affairs ensuring that the self-improvement process continues. Gratitude provides a system of checks and balances by maintaining and preserving the preceding virtues, and allowing continued growth and evolution. Gratitude provides continuation, persistence, growth, expansion, endurance, and intensification. Focused upon last, it is, in reality, at the beginning as well as on the sides supporting, ensuring, and guarding the entire development process

GRATITUDE Sustaining Virtue
Express gratitude generously and receive gratitude humbly and graciously; expect gratitude rarely if ever.

William Arthur Ward (1921-1994)

Gratitude and wrath are both about communication. A decision is made to communicate appreciation to all and for all, or to communicate anger and resentment to all. What is the difference between the most hallowed prayer of thanksgiving and the most vile of verbal tongue lashings? What is the difference between the kindest act of service as opposed to the cruelest act of inhumanity? Both are extreme: one with words and the other with behaviors. Both are driven from deep-seated emotion. Both are intense, high-energy communications. Both radically affect those on the receiving end of the exchange. Reflecting back on the humility and pride discussions, the pivotal moment regarding communication is directly affected by the degree of recognition a person has for others. This is followed by the degree of acceptance of responsibility this person has for the relationships created with others. It becomes a matter of being people-centered and expressing gratitude openly, as opposed to being self-centered and allowing unregulated thoughts, anger, and rage to envelop everyone. It is an issue of allowing positive or negative energy to dominate, and it is witnessed through communication with others.

Maintaining an attitude of gratitude can improve psychological, emotional, and physical well-being. Feelings of gratitude lead to more energy, increased optimism, better social connections, and greater happiness when compared with those who do not consistently feel or express gratitude. Grateful people are less likely to be depressed, envious, greedy, or addicted. From my experience, grateful people sleep more soundly, exercise more regularly, and have greater resistance to illness. These benefits are not restricted by age. Children and young people who feel and act grateful tend to be less materialistic, get better grades, set higher goals, complain of fewer headaches and stomach aches, and feel more satisfied with their friends, families, and school experiences. Feeling grateful or appreciative for someone or something actually attracts more of the same behaviors and circumstances that you appreciate and value. Giving thanks can be beneficial to both the giver and the receiver. It is an acknowledgment that expresses kindness and contentment.

In opposition to gratitude is wrath, which in anger and rage that can lead to cruelty. Anger and wrath are impulsive, and they block gratitude. Anger is often mistakenly associated with toughness and strength. In dealing with anger, some of us seek catharsis by giving it free reign, while others attempt to repress it resulting in bitterness and cynicism. Anger can be manifest as impatience, unkindness, spite, revenge, vigilantism, and cruelty to others. When wrath is directed inward, it becomes self-destructive, violent, and hate full; it can lead to suicide.

At some point in our lives we all experience feelings of anger. Learning to harness these feelings is one of the most important skills to achieve for optimum physical and emotional health. In Psalms, King Solomon counseled us to "cease from anger and forsake wrath." When angry, none of us thinks clearly. We make rash decisions that are later regretted. Anger can be triggered by truly threatening things like an encounter with an assailant, or by something small like a billing error from a cell phone provider. In either case, the nervous system reacts the same way: hormone levels increase, breathing gets faster, pulse increases, blood pressure rises, sweat appears, and pupils dilate. Even headaches may emerge. Blood surges to muscles in preparation for "fight or flight." This deprives the brain of needed oxygen-rich blood resulting in short-sighted reasoning.

In prehistoric times, this "fight or flight" reaction was enormously helpful because it put the body on hyper-alert so that action was imminent. In our modern, fast-paced, aggressive world we still experience this same reaction when our body gets all hyped up. The difference now is that often there is no outlet to channel this energy into, and the frequent triggering of anger increases blood pressure and can actually damage the heart.

To control anger, we must train our minds to pause so that we can think rationally through the things that have or are happening before choosing the proper action. In this way, we consciously choose our actions rather than unconsciously reacting to fearful situations. We must learn to be conscious of what is causing our feelings of anger because strong emotions tend to blind us to the real root of what is bothering us. When angry, none of us thinks clearly, and rash decisions follow. If instead we are able to channel our energy into planning and problem solving, we will see the solutions without getting caught up in bitterness and anger. We will begin to see the good even in difficult circumstances.

All virtues can be strengthened through the implementation of gratitude. Gratitude is the power behind wisdom and peace. It sustains the process of acquiring these virtues, ensuring that they will not diminish. It also completes the cycle of the 8 Virtues, reminding us of the need for continuous self-monitoring and improvement at all levels by expressing thanks for all circumstances. Gratitude enables us to remain humble. By living the preceding virtues of humility, courage, cleanliness, obedience, industry, integrity and wisdom, one's mind, body, and moral fiber are strong enough to ensure that valuable and available effort and time be filled with positive adventures and projects.

Gratitude is an action. As we acknowledge those who have touched our lives, we experience humility and interdependence. Delivering thanks in person can be particularly powerful. Mother Teresa taught the importance of even the simplest act of gratitude: "We will never know all the good that a simple smile can do."

Gratitude, as with all the virtues is a gradual progression of refinement. The gratitude progression begins with the outward expression of appreciation for the positive things in our lives. It is followed by gratitude for the positive, as well as the challenges in our lives. The culminating state of gratitude is one of genuine respect and appreciation for all circumstances confronted.

The gratitude progression includes:

1. <u>Gratitude for the Positive</u>. This is behavior that can be witnessed by others. It is easy to be happy when positive things happen, and grateful behavior is a logical consequence of this. Through societal pressure and protocol, this form of gratitude is expected and rewarded. Outward expressions of thankfulness bring with them a certain degree of satisfaction. Openly expressed appreciation for visibly identifiable gifts enhances self-esteem and social value.
2. <u>Gratitude for Challenges</u>. This behavior is partially identifiable from outward behavior as when challenges come and a positive countenance is maintained. What isn't seen is the transformation within the heart and mind. It is here that a resolution has been established, resulting in positive attitudes and behaviors even when confronted with challenges. Not only do outsiders see the maturity of an individual, but more importantly personal self-esteem is generated within as actions align to words.
3. <u>Gratitude for Everything</u>. This level of gratitude is indeed visible to the onlooker, but the true majesty of this attainment flows from within as the individual's will is transcended. Motivations come from a higher source greater than direct benefit to the individual. Gratitude is offered because it is right, genuine, and heartfelt. Self-esteem flows unrestrained from a Higher Source, and serenity is witnessed from a person's smile to his/her walk.

Gratitude MOTTO:

"The platitude of gratitude is an attitude of thanks."

Mark each statement:

1 never, 2 occasionally, 3 often, 4 frequently, 5 always

_____ *I tell people that I care and appreciate them.*

_____ *I think daily about what others have done for me.*

_____ *I am thankful for my circumstances.*

_____ *I say positive things about other people.*

_____ *I look for the opportunity to serve other people.*

_____ *I am sincerely grateful for the positive impact of others.*

What is the SUSTAINING virtue?

Gratitude is an action providing a system of checks and balances for the proceeding virtues. Focused upon last, it is, in reality, at the beginning as well.

Chapter 10

What is the GOAL?

- *The reward of these efforts is PEACE.*
- *Peace is a state of tranquility and harmony free of cognitive dissonance.*
- *Peace is harmony and inner calm with the physical, the emotional, and the metaphysical.*
- *Fear rises out of perceived feelings of isolation, scarcity, and security; this defeats peace.*
- *Peace is NOT an absolute point of arrival, a state of absence, or a state of possession.*
- *Peace is a sliding scale of various levels of tranquility.*

The <u>Reward</u> for these efforts is Peace. Peace is the capstone of the edifice. Placed there for safety and protection, the roof is the final element of the structure. Peace is the crowning achievement of life, the final stroke of the brush. It must include peace with self, peace with the environment, and peace with fellow travelers through the journey of life. The peak achievement occurs when peace is experienced. Despite the trials and travails of the human experience, personal peace is attainable. To attain this, the greatest of all achievements, each of us must change our natures.

PEACE MUST BE OUR PURPOSE!

**How do you want to create peace
if there is no peace inside yourself?**
Thich Nhat Hanh (1926 -)

As evidenced through the media, our culture doesn't really promote healthy feelings about ourselves. I've determined that this world is a rough, demanding, and unsafe place, and consequently it is easy to feel insecure, discontented, and dissatisfied. Sadly, it's all about the vanity of deficiencies: what I don't have, what I lack, what I'm missing, who's winning, and why I am not. All of this competition leads to feeling anything but peaceful.

It's been said that we become like those things we admire. By placing our values on the wrong things we become disillusioned. For as long as I can remember, owning things has been promoted as the goal for feeling successful and fulfilled. Having access to lots of money is sold as the ultimate objective of life. The problem with this type of reasoning is that we never own enough of anything. The average person has lost perspective of what is truly important. Money is not a substitute for security, control is not a substitute for safety, and power is not a substitute for tenderness. Personal peace cannot be purchased.

What is peace? It's a journey, it's a right, it's a gift, and it grows only when we share it. Peace is a state of tranquility and harmony free of oppression, unpleasant thoughts, and emotions. Peace is harmony in all relationships: physical, emotional, and metaphysical. Peace is an inner sense of calm. It comes from becoming still so that we can reflect and meditate upon our inner wisdom, and receive answers from the unseen. Peace is letting go of what we cannot control. In acceptance there is peace as ill thoughts are released. A peaceful heart is one that is free from worry and fear. Peace is a conscience free of inconsistencies, hypocrisy, dishonesty, and deceit. When our soul is quiet we can more clearly understand issues, and are more open to creative solutions; this allows us to live in the present. Peace is not a distant goal that we seek, but a means by which we can arrive at the goal.

True stability rests on issues more enduring than current matters. Peace can be found in the storm, calmness can be felt during the fight, and security can be achieved in the heat of battle. Fear, however, defeats peace because it rises out of feelings of isolation and scarcity; it destroys our perspective of security. Anger also opposes peace as it manifests itself in a series of non-communicated fears generated internally. Hostility, wrath, and revenge are responses to this perceived fear. When adrenaline does the thinking, our emotions will flow with the chemical tide. Frenzied feelings of paranoia, anxiety, and trauma are easily imagined during such times. This agitated feeling seems to be more the norm in society today rather than the exception. Sometimes we become so extreme and fearful that we are offended or threatened over everything. We lash out in defense before even attempting to understand a situation. All of this opposes personal peace.

To offend is human, but to take offense when none is intended is foolish. Understanding leads to peace. Misunderstanding is based in miscommunication and leads to fear. Often threats to personal peace and tranquility are perceptions in the mind rather than realities. A Japanese proverb states "Fear is only as deep as the mind will allow." We communicate by word, text, and behavior. Meanings to these communications are in the people, their circumstance, and their history. Meanings are not in words alone. The wise Native American challenges us to "walk a mile in my moccasins." Anxiety, fear, and intimidation all have at their core misunderstanding rising from miscommunication. There are few demons out there who justify the fear we attribute to them. Our challenge lies in communicating compassion and harmony.

Personal Peace

Peace is a state of mental calmness resulting in emotional stability. Peace is the absence of mental conflict. Peace is honesty to self: honesty in word, deed, thought, and motive. Our world has devolved to a state of "the end justifies the means." Fiduciary responsibility is today's business integrity. Many are left with addictions for success and the resultant guilt of untallied costs. This is cognitive dissonance at its finest. To be peaceable, we must learn to be at peace with ourselves. Holding conflicting ideas in our minds prevents the regenerating power of wisdom from taking hold. To love we must be lovable, and if we have felt the sting of rejection it will require a conscious, sustained effort to accept self and risk trusting again. Personal enlightenment is merely recognition of this perspective. Love is real. It is pure energy. As an eternal creation it cannot be destroyed but only buried. Nothing real can be threatened, and nothing unreal exists, so love poured out abundantly can squelch all fear. Given this reasoning I conclude that our journey through life is really quite simple: it is merely the acceptance of pure love back into our lives through the giving and receiving of reciprocal kindness.

As newborn babies we all were initially filled with love. Fear is what we learn while interacting with each other. It is a natural byproduct of insufficient knowledge. Linked to ego, fear has its purpose: it is directly tied to personal accomplishments and performances as we stand up to challenges, but once attained, fear of loss quickly follows as do vanity, greed, and envy. The reality is that all humanity possesses inherent merit regardless of performance. Your very existence validates your worth.

Peace, therefore, is a state of mind. As an intangible, it is a desired situation but one that is only validated through feelings. True global peace can only be attained as suffering ends, and as such it should be a goal for all humanity. Personal inner peace is earned over time through discipline and self-control. It is perceived as a state of bliss, happiness, serenity and calmness. To be a peaceful person one ensures that even when encountering strong emotions, hurt or anger, these feelings are controlled and not amplified. Peace is calmness in any and all circumstances, settings, and situations. People can be at peace even in physical bondage and, conversely, being free does not ensure peace. All of us have felt the sensation of inner peace at one time or another. Illusive and transient, our fast-paced lives are in direct opposition to inner peace. All the wealth in the world cannot purchase true inner peace; it is achieved without money and often alluded because of money.

Personal inner peace can be witnessed outwardly by others. People at peace are calmer, their countenance is lighter, and their speech and mannerisms are more reflective. Peace, like wisdom, is a gift that is fleeting and occasional. The harder one strives for it, the longer it lingers. Over time, peace infuses our lives as fewer things are perceived as traumatic. Anxiety also diminishes in direct proportion and a sense of enlightenment emerges. Again the 8 Virtues Authenticity Assessment is a great way to check personal progress.

Why is peace so rare, so fragile, so tenuous, and so easily disrupted? How can we become more like the yogi who lie on beds of nails or walk on white-hot coals and receive no bodily harm, but are able to remain peaceful and tranquil throughout? Peace is more than the opposite of war. Gandhi's admonition, "There is no way to peace; peace is the way," aligns to that of Buddha: "Do not seek the peace without, peace comes from within." What is this inner peace Gandhi and Buddha advocate? How do we achieve it and sustain it? What challenges calmness, serenity and tranquility? What annoying, distressing, irritating, antagonizing, or disruptive events spoil our peace? Irritants are everywhere and they beg us to react to them, to focus upon them, and to concentrate on their urgent cry. Instead we must eliminate these distractions from our consciousness.

Peace Progression

The opposite of peace is fear. Fear includes feelings of stress, anxiety, guilt, or suffering that bring about a state of dissatisfaction; all of these sensations are fear-based. It is an uncomfortable place, that of falling short of desires, expectations, and plans. Like peace, dissatisfaction is of the mind. Suffering is part of the world and it results from misplaced desires which become an entangled web of unmet needs. To overcome feelings of dissatisfaction we must be smart about what we desire. The only way to do this is by controlling our thoughts, and so change comes from within. Just as suffering comes from suffering in the mind, and violence comes from violence in the mind, so peace comes from peace in the mind. Peace is a state of satisfaction as we learn to control our desires.

WHEN YOU FEEL AT PEACE	WHEN YOU DON'T FEEL AT PEACE
You feel happy, calm, and clear of mind.	You feel unhappy, depressed, confused, frustrated, and fearful.
You feel generous towards others.	You feel possessive, self-centered, resentful, and greedy.
You don't get offended.	You are easily offended.
You let everyone see what you are doing.	You become secretive and evasive.
You want to be with people and make them happy.	You avoid family and friends.
You are glad to help others.	You avoid helping others.
You feel like meditating.	You don't meditate.
You feel in control: don't overeat, oversleep, lose temper, or have uncontrolled passion or desire.	You feel out of control: excessive emotion, fear, hate, envy, anger, lust, hunger, and fatigue.
You feel confident and glad you are alive.	You are easily discouraged and let fears override reason.

We don't arrive at a state of tranquility over night. It is something that can take a lifetime. It is a slow, calculated change of nature.

Often peace begins with nothing more than a desire for quietude. Something must cause us to wake up and arouse our consciousness. Something must instill inside us the yearning to experiment with it. Look upon it as a seed planted within the heart. Once planted, the seed will grow. If it is a good seed it will produce positive effects. These positive effects will in turn lead to the development of greater inner peace. After time, random occasional episodes of peaceful tranquility will give way to deliberate and conscious efforts, and subsequent periods including scheduled prayer and meditation. The craving for this serenity will begin to swell within as understanding expands and reason flourishes. These enlightened periods will become more frequent and longer in duration as personal awareness expands and the mind awakens. Like the young plant, nutrients and care are required as it takes root. With time it matures and begins to bear fruit. If neglected under the heat of the sun it will wither and die. On the other hand, diligence, patience, and care results in fruit for all to share. As with the seed, a profound change of nature toward peace will be a blessing to all who are near and dear.

Various forms of training such as prayer, meditation, or yoga cultivate inner peace. Peace is not an absolute point of arrival, not a discrete state of absence or possession, but a sliding scale of variable levels of tranquility. The peace progression advocated here can be identified as three distinct levels of attainment. The initial state is one of random and occasional occurrences or episodes of peace. This unpredictable state of peace is followed by deliberate, planned, and executed periods of peace. Continual peace is achieved as larger and more frequent durations are enjoyed because the stresses, anxieties, and fears of daily life are managed and controlled. Anxiety and peace cannot co-exist for as one increases the other decreases.

The peace progression includes:

1. <u>Random Peace</u>. Occasional random occurrences and episodes of stillness, quiet, and calm. These moments typically end abruptly as external events overcome the silence. These periods are recognized, appreciated, and enjoyed but are random and therefore unmanageable. Others can tell when we are feeling peace because of the calmness of our countenance. Fear is minimized.
2. <u>Deliberate Peace</u>. This includes scheduled, predictable periods of undisturbed silence and serenity as with yoga, meditation, and prayer. A conscious effort is allocated daily to such activities, resulting in greater moments of tranquility. As with any skill, the more practice the greater the proficiency. Identifiable behavior changes are acknowledged. Fear has become a stranger.
3. <u>Continual Peace</u>. This state includes the absence of conflicting ideas through pre-determined and practiced integrity. Fearlessness and enlightenment are achieved as longer and more frequent durations of peace are enjoyed. This occurs when the yearning for this serene state of being becomes greater than any and all other competitors for our time. All

people encountered are benefactors of this state of enlightenment and tranquility.

The children of the world are indeed our future. In them lie the seeds for change. In them rests the power for good. In them sleeps the strength to direct. Through them the potential of humanity expands. They will follow our example whatever it may be. All of us are connected to a child in some way, either directly or indirectly. We have an immediate influence on them through our examples. We have a responsibility to them. Currently, people of the world are floundering in the derailing vices of vanity, cowardice, lust, gluttony, sloth, greed, wrath, and envy. Fear dominates the media's message. These behaviors are in direct opposition to peace. As peace becomes our purpose we can more easily stand as a witness to the children within our influence by being a positive example of the virtues that lead directly to a peaceful life.

Peace should be the crowning achievement of our existence, the final stroke or the culmination of our work. We seek for peace with self, peace with the earth and environment, and peace with everyone and everything in the world.

Peace begins with a smile.
Mother Teresa (1910-1997)

Mark each statement:

1 never, 2 occasionally, 3 often, 4 frequently, 5 always

_____ *I feel peaceful and optimistic about the future.*

_____ *I am kind and patient with others.*

_____ *I find joy in others achievements.*

_____ *My greatest desires is to be at peace with myself, neighbors and environment.*

_____ *I love and cherish principles of peace and virtue.*

_____ *I have no desire to be mean, but to be kind to all.*

What is the GOAL?

Peace is the crowning achievement of life. Peace with others follows peace with your environment, beginning and ending with peace with yourself. Wise people desire and strive for peace. By example, peaceful people are the best teachers of virtues.

Chapter 11

What is the program?

We paint the story of our lives by the choices we make. Life is about improving our strengths rather than envying those of others.
Grandpa Seamonster (First and Last, Slow and Fast)

> - *A return to virtuous living with the goal of personal peace is paramount.*
> - *Young people today must ask, "Where do I, as an individual, fit into the global competition and opportunities of the day?"*
> - *This program offers an unwavering foundation for children and young people to enable then to adapt, adjust and flourish in this ever-changing, increasingly complex, and demanding world.*

The Evolution of SamiTales

As we age and surpass mid-life, it is a common feeling to want to give back to society, and to leave a legacy of good that will outlast us. We often get involved in humanitarian efforts and local service or volunteer initiatives. When Karen and I married we shared such ideals, and began researching where we could best serve society given our rich and varied education and professional experience.

In the course of this exploration, Karen began to read through a large collection of my personal reflections written over a number of years as I worked through a series of life experiences. As she read, she concluded that several of these reflections stood out as having the potential to become exceptional children's storybooks. She proceeded to edit and refine the words until they were ready for illustrations. Where could we find an illustrator who would adequately capture the tender feelings and emotions of the author? She suggested that I make initial sketches, after which a "real" illustrator could be hired. To our delight, the retro look of the illustrations weren't bad and so we continued forward.

By the time I had illustrated the third book, we realized that something was missing from the cute human faces. We decided to move to animals, and the logical choice was a seamonster because of our last name: Seamons. Acting upon Karen's vision, I began to develop the Seamonster Family. We did some research to see how common this creature was in children's literature, and found it to be a fresh, new character who could also promote a strong environmental theme.

In the storybook, *Son of My Son*, there is an illustration of Grandpa Seamonster teaching young Sami as they sit on a precipice in the deep waters of the lake led us to uncover the 8 Virtues. We talked at length about what words or concepts a grandparent would use to teach and prepare a young, impressionable grandchild for the challenges and joys of life. Before long we had a series of eight words that we considered vitally important to achieving a happy and productive life. As we continued to meditate and dialogue over these words, we recognized that they were all time-proven virtues that wise minds from every walk of life, past and present, had promoted as the path to peace. It was discovered that the 8 Virtues could be ordered in such a way as to be additive and hierarchical. It appeared that the first five were the common path to achieving success, but no matter how great one's achievements, success did not guarantee peace of mind. While success requires honesty to society through obedience to laws, peace of mind is only attainable through honesty to self. The sixth virtue of integrity is the point of decision leading to peace. Unknowingly, we had stumbled upon something that is sorely needed in our world today: virtue training.

As an educator and author, Karen became immersed in the potential. Grounded in these newly organized topics, her mind began to race. One after another the stories developed. She was barely through with one and three other stories would appear. As she wrote, it became necessary to define the topics more clearly and to refine the program. The Child of Virtue manual is the result of her questions. This text, What About Me? was added as a reader-friendly, condensed version.

As she wrote, the issue of reading level became a topic of discussion. It was determined to develop manuscripts that stretched the reader's abilities. This led to the creation of the Reader Reference User Guide at the end of each book. Challenging words needed to be defined, probing questions offered, and real world applications suggested. To our surprise we had developed a whole new style of children's literature.

The motto, "Child of Virtue, Peace is My Purpose," came to us one day over lunch. It came with such force that it literally propelled us forward as we began developing ideas and concepts of how to reach and teach virtuous living to children the world over. Going through this process has been personally painful, however, because of the topics and concepts that have brought us face to face with who we are, not who we thought we were. SamiTales is the happy result of this adventure, and we are excited to be part of such a life-changing journey.

SamiTales Program of 8 Virtues Training

The world's a scary place! To quote Charles Dickens from a Tale of Two Cities, "It was the best of times. It was the worst of times, it was the age of wisdom, it was the age of foolishness." Profound changes are in progress; national, cultural and physical barriers of the past are falling daily. Things will never be the same. To combat this volatile and potentially dangerous situation, a return to virtuous living with the goal of personal peace, is paramount. Personal peace leads to peace in the home, community, nation, and eventually the world.

World peace begins in the mind. World peace begins in the home. World peace begins with virtue training! How do we get global, time proven, non-denominational, society-stabilizing virtue training to every child on the planet? It starts with a simple slogan: "Child of Virtue, Peace is my Purpose!"

Today's technology-fueled shrinking world is confronting children with unprecedented complexity demanding tolerance and connectivity. Instead of asking, "Where does my country fit into the world economy?" young people today must ask, "Where do I, as an individual, fit into the global competition and opportunities of the day?" This is demanding greater maturity at a much younger age than in any previous era. Building on the shoulders of the past, today's children possess the capacity to absorb and internalize advanced topics much earlier, but many are constrained by traditional institutions and paradigms.

SamiTales and 8 Virtues Training provide a bridge between two dynamic forces:
1. the worldwide need for value-based training,
2. the advent of digital e-books, social networking and downloadable smartphone apps resulting in the availability of electronic media to virtually everyone on the plant.

SamiTales and the 8 Virtues Program provide an unwavering foundation for children and young people to enable them to adapt, adjust, and flourish in this ever-changing, increasingly complex, and demanding world. We believe that virtue training will result in greater self-mastery leading to lower levels of aggression and higher social affiliation that will produce happier, more stress-free lives.

The 8 Virtues are time proven and culturally independent. They are not novel, difficult or evasive, but rather straight forward, readily available, and attainable through consistent attention and diligence. This program is aimed at teaching children to not only survive in this world, but to thrive. The mission is to provide assistance with these age old techniques and ideals to aid in the pursuit of peace: personal peace, environmental peace, and world peace. This peace is achieved through managed pride and fostered humility. This support helps youth catch the vision of self mastery and success through delayed gratification, courage, cleanliness, obedience, and industry leading to peace through personal integrity, wisdom, and gratitude.

Child of Virtue

MISSION: To inspire people throughout the world to embrace a life of continuous improvement leading to personal peace by incorporating time proven virtues into their own lives, and by teaching and modeling such behaviors to all children whom they can influence.

VISION: We exist to enhance children's sensitivity, skills, and understanding to enable them to adapt to the demands of and to thrive in our dynamically changing world. We believe that by capturing and sustaining a child's attention, we can educate them. Through a global perspective, we delight children and adults alike through laughter, universal challenges and wholesome entertainment as they share in the birth and life experiences of a baby seamonster. We established Little Ones Of Promise (LOOP), a 501(c)(3) non-profit organization to enhance the education and advancement of at-risk children worldwide.

OBJECTIVE: To create an organized curriculum consisting of a series of children's books, reader references, instructional materials and other related media, based upon the principles of virtuous living, and presented through the relationships and experiences of Sami Seamonster and his family and friends. The 8 Virtues are embedded into the SamiTales stories through the development of common childhood experiences that address each virtue. Additional topics will include hard issues such as death, abuse, and tragedy. Environmental issues such as pollution, global warming, and natural disasters, and animal rights issues such as endangerment and extinction will also be addresses.

Through entertaining, captivating, and educationally sound curriculum, books, and media, these foundational virtues and globally demanding skills are presented to preschool, home school, and K-6 children of all cultures. This training is instructionally sound with a fresh setting, adorable characters, and green themes. Free online curriculum (childofvirtue.com) and instructor materials, with a blog link (samitalesblogspot.com) for user contributions, are also provided.

Through the common childhood experiences of Sami Seamonster, readers are taught the importance of living a virtuous life with the end result of personal peace. Story books in the SamiTales Series validate and provide simple, yet powerful, examples of virtues and virtue training. At the end of each storybook, a Reader's Reference User Guide is included. Difficult vocabulary words are defined in the context of the story, environmental issues are described, and reflective questions are provided to promote critical thinking about the various topics. These questions can be adapted to provide further explanation and discussion with younger children, or as actual assignments with older children.

The reading level and advanced topics presented in these books can challenge even adult experience. They are designed to be read at a variety of levels with open dialogue between adult and child. They are adapted according to audience and specific need. Additional readings will enable deeper thought and personal reflection. The ultimate goal is a commitment to virtuous living leading to personal peace.

Example is a powerful teacher. More important than what is taught to these hungry young minds is how you, the teacher, live. The 8 Virtue Attribute Assessment, introduced in Chapter 1, is an ongoing reality check in the process of discovering self. Its value is tied directly to personal honesty and continued use.

What is the program?

The SamiTales / 8 Virtues Program is aimed at teaching children to not only survive in this world but to thrive.

Chapter 12

What can I do?

Do all the good you can, by all the means you can, in all the ways you can, in all the places you can, at all the times you can, to all the people you can, as long as ever you can.
John Wesley (1703-1791)

- *Reactions to momentary demands determine your destiny and validate the objects of your affection.*
- *We are either getting closer to or farther away from our potential.*
- *Until a person is committed there is a sense of reluctance, hesitancy, and the possibility of withdrawal all of which ensures ineffectiveness.*
- *Become part of this great work! You will be blessed with peace in your personal life, greater peace in your neighborhood, and in time you will feel the difference in the world.*

"Too soon old, too old smart" is a simple Italian proverb I came across years ago, but it wasn't until recently that I allowed the significance of this sentiment to settle in. It now reminds me that life, in fact, is short and that in its briefness, the sooner I understand myself, the happier will be the outcome. I am discovering that the more wisdom I obtain, the more exposed are my flaws. Left unchecked, cognitive dissonance leads to anxiety as these two competing concepts converge. I must accept myself or who I am, where I am, and who I desire to become. Too often, close associates, including family and friends, hold us to past lives and performances. I can either wallow away in regret for past mistakes, or resolve to adjust, improve, and press forward. Guilt must be replaced with sorrow leading to action.

Life is pretty straightforward. Cutting through the noise and distractions that enclose us, at the end of the day it is all about whom and what dominates personal thought. In the idle times, where do our minds migrate? When resting, who or what consumes our vision? If individual sensory satisfaction is at our core, then all thoughts and behaviors will support that end. Attempting to refocus thought is admirable, but the true test comes when the unexpected knocks. Engaged in a quest of self importance, is the call for assistance met with annoyance or prospect? Be it a beggar in want of food or the homeless in need of shelter, reactions to the momentary demands placed in our path will determine personal destiny, document individual focus, and measure the object of our affection. These unconscious reactions unveil our true veiled focus. When the moment appears to serve, am I irritated, guilt-ridden, or grateful? Or worse yet, do I miss these subtle, yet decisive, opportunities due to a hectic or urgently demanding routine?

Over time my focus is set, and it is not easily returned back to a previous state of simplicity. The ego, in its most barbaric ways, conspires to enslave us all. We become personally invested with the pride of possession and accomplishment. An identified deeper attachment develops that can be acknowledged as selfishness and vanity. Truth humbly retires before the arrogant, and no eternal matters are accessible until freedom of focus is attained. The human mind at its base order is crawling with countless world delusions. Struggles in the battlefield pale in significance when compared to these inner enemies. The timid refuse the conflict for they conclude that by acquiring nothing, they have nothing to renounce. Only when we have battled and won can we enrich the world by bestowing the fruits of our profound personal victory to others. By striving, struggling, and growing, each success no matter how small results in less cognitive dissonance creating greater calm within.

Each moment of our life we are coming closer to or falling further from our potential. Yet, as we arrive near the end, we begin to see how much has been missed along the way. Each day we should learn something new about the world, and in so doing we will never be the same as we currently are. We should celebrate the limitless capacity that we each possess to learn, to grow, and to achieve. A basic law of nature states: that which does not grow dies. A life trapped in well-worn paths of habits and routines is greatly limited. The human mind is a miracle as each new idea creates an entirely new thought or concept. It is limitless, restrained only by personal fears of safety and security. Our self-defined boundaries and limits pre-mark our growth. Listen to the possibilities as we together state, "I don't know the answer but together let's find out." Together with our fellow travelers on this earth we can share the journey by unraveling the mysteries and exploring the wonders that are everywhere.

What is left? Where to turn? When to move? How to proceed? Who to touch? It is the shadow of our souls, the façade of our beings, and the pretense of our lives that loses responsiveness to the woes of others. Indecision is debilitating and habit-forming. Like a contagious disease, it transmits itself to others. Laying aside the selfish desires and ambitions of self-interest to freely bestow what you have in your hand without question or anticipation of gain and never flinch from misunderstanding, is what the authentic soul desires. We must ensure that we place ourselves in situations that promote the good of humanity. This includes all living forces, and not just the popular, fashionable, admired, or trendy. From the jobs we accept to the activities attended, a conscious determination to be an influence for good regardless of the magnitude, regardless of the notoriety, and regardless of the reward, is what we seek. Mindfully striving to make more deposits toward the human cause than withdrawals from it, enables us to cheerfully endure with a trust that in the end all things will work together for our good.

As I sit back and reflect upon the media's portrayal of the world and its attendant danger, evil, injuries, and threats, I ask myself, "What can I do to help? What can I do to ease the pain, comfort the sad, and bring smiles to the children?" Suddenly the sharp piercing voice of a child penetrates my mind and heart. "What can you do to help? Don't ask with the vain rhetoric of the insincere yet socially correct! It's obvious! I'm bleeding to death, can't you see! Look beyond the image of what is typically expected. Avoid the babble of the socially wired. Gaze into my soul. The emptiness, fear, and pain is there; can't you see it? Pick something, any of the multiple of challenges you see. Do it without fanfare or praise. Your reward is this memory engraved into my soul for eternity. The warmth, the embrace, and the security of knowing you cared enough to think of me specifically. Although you might not heal all known injuries, or cure all known diseases, today, right now you did something for me. I am only one but I will remember you forever." It's not the magnitude or value of the gift that is important. It's the conscious selection and warmth of the hand of the giver that determines its true eternal worth.

Until a person is committed there is a sense of reluctance, hesitancy, and the chance to withdraw, all of which ensures ineffectiveness. All acts of initiative and creation pivot upon this one elementary truth. Its significance is usually ignored, resulting in the death of countless ideas and plans. It isn't until the moment one definitely commits, that providence moves forward. A whole stream of events issue from that first decision, all of which work in one's favor, including the obstacles. From unforeseen incidents and meetings with key influential individuals to material assistance, when help is needed it will come. German author Goethe is attributed with saying, "Whatever you can dream, you can do. Boldness has genius, power and magic in it."

Children: A DECLARATION of Rights

We, the children of the world, desire to feel safe and secure so that we can learn and grow without fear. We desire peace so that we can develop our talents, progress, and become part of something important. We desire to have families and homes, and to work and play in harmony. We know that peace begins with us, and so we commit to build personal character. We know that world peace begins and is sustained with inner peace. We must conquer the angry soul, both within and without, through love, not revenge.

We the children of the world desire:
- Someone to care for me
- Someone to protect me
- Someone to lead me
- Someone to guide me
- Someone to teach me
- Someone to encourage me
- Someone to love me

Peace is my birthright!

MOMs: A DECLARATION to the World

We believe it is important to work for the betterment of humanity and the planet. We are determined to use our knowledge and skills to this end. We know that one woman or one man can make a difference in the lives of many.

We the MOMs of the world commit:
- To listen to a child daily
- To read to a child daily
- To hug a child daily

MOMMIES ARE FOREVER

We define the title of MOM broadly to include all women and men who are committed to nurturing children. This is more than a genetic relationship. The call for MOMs is a call to all people worldwide regardless of age, nationality, religion, marital status, or economic standing. A child's only desire is that you spend time with him/her, and show them your love. Our call to MOMs everywhere is a declaration to reach out and emotionally adopt a child in need.

A MOM is a nurturer, but we don't stop there because nurturers can be anyone. Nurturers possess a common set of characteristics, the foundation of which resides in developing young people. This quality is so powerful, so critical, and so imperative in the formulation of the child's sense of being that without it the child emotionally withers and dies. Home is where the child's personal sense of worth is established. It grows to affect the neighborhood, and then to influence the world. As such, we invite you to begin serving children wherever you are. If there is joy and satisfaction in serving one of these little ones of promise, how great will be your joy and fulfillment in serving many. Don't stop. You're never too old; you're never too young. "MOMMIES ARE FOREVER."

Become part of this marvelous work! We need you! You are invited to join this movement by offering whatever you can give. We promise great joy from your efforts. Become engaged in it and your life will change for the better. The things that matter most in life are not the costly. Share your time with someone starving for attention, someone hungry to learn, and someone craving affection. Sharing of time demonstrates love while spending of means demonstrates wealth; only you can choose what you will give. The reality of life involves managing personal time and setting goals. The measure of a "quality life" is to spend time on the things that matter most. Nothing, yes nothing, is of greater worth than the minds and hearts of the rising generation.

There is no greater worth, no greater gift, and no greater cause than that of loving one child daily, consistently, and without condition. By committing to just five minutes a day of unconditional, unobstructed time, after 52 weeks you will have been part of a miracle. You will have changed a life forever. Five minutes a day equates to 25 hours a year. Three hundred and sixty five individual moments of development, security, and growth is galactically greater than one day of intense fun.

We need your help. We urgently need your love, your longing for renewal, and your desire for higher ground. We need your arms to hug, your lips to speak, your ears to listen, and your hearts to care. These small children need to hear, see, and feel your compassion. They need examples of goodness and empathy. They need the nurturing that only you can give. Let us all be part of this great work! You will be blessed with peace in your personal life, greater peace in your neighborhood, and in time you will feel the difference in the world.

We express our heartfelt gratitude for considering our offer and we look forward to assisting you in changing your world.

What can I do?

It isn't until the moment one definitely commits that providence moves forward. When help is needed it will come. We look forward to assisting you in changing your world.

**Yesterday is gone, tomorrow has not come;
we have only today, let us begin.**
Mother Teresa (1910-1997)

**Visit us at
www.childofvirtue.com**

References

Albom, Mitch. (1997) Tuesdays With Morrie. Doubleday.

Allen, James. (1902) As A Man Thinketh. Bookcraft.

Ausubel, D. (1968) Educational Psychology: A Cognitive View. Holt, Rhinehart & Winston.

Bloom, B.S. (1968) Learning for Mastery. University of California, Berkeley.

Bruner, J.S. (1966) Towards a Theory of Instruction. Norton.

Dante, A. The Divine Comedy. First published in 1472.

Deming, E. (1950) Lectures to Union of Japanese Scientists and Engineers.

Farrington, D.P. (2002) 'Development criminology and focused prevention' in M. Maquire The Oxford handbook of Criminology (3rd ed). Oxford: Oxford University Press.

Frankl, V.E. (1947) Man's Search for Meaning. Washington Square Press.

Gagne, R.M. (1985) The Conditions of Learning 4th Edition. Holt, Rinehart & Winston.

Herzberg, F. (1966) Work and the Nature of Man. World Printing.

Jung, C.G. (1971) Psychology Types. Princeton University Press.

Kohlberg, L. (1981) Psychology of Moral Development. Harper Row.

Lambert, M. (1983) New Course Planning: The strategy and tactics of developing a home study course. Natural Home Study Press.

Lewis, C.S. (1963) What Christians Believe. Harper.

Livinston, Gordon. (2004) Too Soon Old, Too Late Smart. Marlow & Co.

Maslow, A. H. (1954) Motivation and Personality. Harper & Row.

Pausch, Randy. (2008) The Last Lecture. Hyperion Books.

Piaget, J. (1952) The Origins of Intelligence in Infants. Norton.

Strauss, W. & Howe, N. (2000) *Millennials Rising: The Next Generation.*

Sickmund, M., TJ Sladky, & Wei Kang (2008). *"Census of Juveniles in Residential Placement Databook" [Online].* Washington, DC: US Department of Justice, Office of Juvenile and Delinquency Prevention.

Skinner, B.F. (1971) *Beyond Freedom and Dignity.* Banton.

Travers, R.M.W. (1982) *Essentials for Learning.* Macmillan.

Ulrich, W. (2008) *Forgiving Ourselves.*

Yogananda, Paramahansa. (1946) *Autobiography of Yoga*

Web sites:

www.compassion.com

www.finestquotes.com

www.inspiration-quotes.info

www.motivation-inspirational-corner.com

www.quotationspage.com

www.ingramcontent.com/pod-product-compliance
Lightning Source LLC
Chambersburg PA
CBHW021013090426
42738CB00007B/771